The Best Teen Reads ·2007·

Sharron L. McElmeel

Hi Willow Research & Publishing
2007

Hi Willow Research & Publishing
312 South 1000 East
Salt Lake City UT 84102-2411

Dist. by LMC Source online at: http://www.lmcsource.com

Ordering information:
Electronic orders can be done on the website of LMC Source
Mail orders to:
LMC Source
358 South 700 East #B305
Salt Lake City, UT 84102
lmcsource@comcast.net
Telephone orders to: 800-873-3043
800-225-0540 Fax

ISBN: 1-933170-24-7

Table of Contents

Section 1

The Best Teen Reads

The Best Teen Reads
Introduction

Who decides what are the best teen reads? In this case, the best teen reads are those books published in the recent publishing seasons that have received star reviews from professional reviewing sources or have been tapped as an award winning book in the immediate past year. For the most part the books listed in the following pages are those that were published for and marketed to young adults. The one major exception are those books that are identified as adult books that teens will read and enjoy. Books appearing as award-winning books have, in general, been published the prior year. Those of us considering purchasing and recommending books in 2007–08 will want to look to the most recent best books and choice book lists from 2007 (the 2007 lists are in the process of being compiled by various organizations and publications). The entries in the following booklist have coded references to the lists and professional reviews that we surveyed. We reviewed these lists and identified those that our work with young readers verified as among the best; additional books were identified because of student interviews, press received, and perhaps published too late in the publishing year to receive formal notice.

ALA Best Book: Each year the American Library Association names a list of best books published in the prior year. The previous year's list is posted on line at http://www.ala.org/ala/yalsa/booklistsawards/bestbooksya/bestbooksyoung.htm

Bank Street College of Education Best Book—2004: The Best Books list, selected for more than 90 years, is designed to guide parents, teachers, and librarians in choosing the very best books for children. http://www.bankstreet.edu/bookcom/

BCCB Blue Ribbon Non-fiction Book Award: The Bulletin of the Center for Children's Books issues an annual Blue Ribbon List. The list is available at http://www.lis.uiuc.edu/puboff/bccb/blueindex.html; the 2005 list is available at http://bccb.lis.uiuc.edu/blue05.html

Coretta Scott King Award: An award presented annually during the ALA convention. Only African American writers are eligible. http://www.ala.org/ala/emiert/corettascottkingbookawards

Junior Literary Guild: For over 75 years the Junior Literary Guild has selected "bestsellers" for its guild members. Their selections can be accessed at http://www.literaryguild.com/doc/content/sitelets/Sitelet_Theme_3.jhtml?SID=JL_3

Michael A. Printz Award/Honor: An American Library Association award named for Michael A. Printz. (See Section 6.)

National Book Award for Young People's Literature: The National Book Foundation awards honors adult books and books in the young people's category. http://www.nationalbook.org/

National Council for the Social Studies: Selected by this professional organization as one of the best books of the year. http://www.ncss.org/

Newbery Award/Honor: An American Library Association award named for John Newbery. (See Section 6.)

Nominee for Edgar YA Mystery Award—2004: Each year the Mystery Writers of America nominate books, published in the prior year, in this genre. The award winner is named in April of each year. Various categories are included. http://www.mysterywriters.org/

OSBCB, History/Science—2004: The American Library Association annually names a list of books designated as Outstanding Books for the College Bound and Life-long Learners. Books are designated in various curriculum areas/areas of interest. http://www.ala.org/yalsa/booklists/obcb

Pura Belpré Award/Honor: An American Library Association award. (See Section 6.)

Quick Pick-YA Reluctant Readers: Annually the American Library Association selects titles for its "Quick Picks for Reluctant Young Adult Readers." http://www.ala.org/yalsa/booklists/quickpicks

Robert F. Siebert Award: An award for information books given by the American Library Association. (See Section 6.)

SLJ Adult books for HS 2004: Each year the School Library Journal lists their picks of adult books that will, in the editors' opinion, appeal to high school readers. http://www.schoollibraryjournal.com/

Starred Booklist: Books that received a star review in Booklist (a publication of the ALA), a professional reviewing source. Most Booklist reviews may be read online through the Barnes and Noble book and Amazon.com site, which pay a fee to republish the reviews for your convenience. http://www.ala.org/booklist/

Starred Kirkus: Books that received a star review in Kirkus Reviews, a professional reviewing source. Most Kirkus reviews may be read online through the Barnes and Noble book site, which pays a fee to republish the reviews for your convenience. http://www.kirkusreviews.com

Starred PW: Books that received a star review in Publishers Weekly, a professional reviewing source focused primarily at the bookstore industry. Most Publisher Weekly reviews may be read online through the Amazon.com or the Barnes and Noble book site, which pay a fee to republish the reviews for your convenience.

VOYA Top 10: The top ten books reviewed by The Voice of Youth Advocates. VOYA is a bi-monthly library journal. http://www.voya.com

Identifying exactly what reader, based on age or grade, each of these books is appropriate for is not an exact science. Maturation, reading ability, interest, and need all play a role in identifying appropriate reading material for any individual or group of readers. Every eighth grade reader is not the same as the eighth grade reader sitting in the next chair. In this book we have provided information that will provide some guidelines for appropriate age level. The age of the main characters, number of pages, and content are all indicators of what readers might enjoy in the book. By the time a reader reaches middle school, actual reading levels vary so widely that designating any book for one grade level is simply a guess at best. Selection of books is more compatible with interest in the book's contents. The information included in the annotations that follow present only guidelines as indicators of appropriateness based on subject matter, presentation of the material, and interest. Interest often allows a reader to rise above reading level restrictions to master a book of high interest, while other readers who are more able may wish to read a book at a lower reading level because of interest or a need for information. Thus we leave it to you, the user of this guide, to determine which students might best relate to any particular title.

These books are the best of the best books to consider in 2007 and beyond.

The Best Teen Reads

❑ Abel, Jessica. *La Perdida*. (2006) Random House/Knopf/Pantheon. (0375423656). 288 pgs. Poverty and lack of direction may be serious for young white Americans, but in Mexico, Carla Olivares, a Mexican-American soon discovers that those traits can quickly lead to violence in a country with few resources. Caught up in a kidnapping scheme Carla soon finds out that she has a few things to learn. Graphic Novel. NPR's 2006 Summer Reading List; BBYA (nominated 2007); PW; Booklist

Author Note
Read about Jessica Abel and the background of *La Perdida* by visiting her website at http://jessicaabel.com. Her two-year-long trip to Mexico provided a lot of the information that she incorporated into the story of Carla Olivares's experiences in Mexico. Links will take visitors to more information about *La Perdida* and Abel's other books.

❑ Acampora, Paul. *Defining Dulcie*. (2006) Penguin Group USA/Dial. (0803730462). 176 pgs. Dulcie, her father, and her grandfather are all janitors at the local Connecticut high school. But when Dulcie's father dies from fumes, her mother packs up and moves herself and Dulcie to California, leaving the grief behind. But Dulcie wants to remember her father and longs for her old comfortable life. Taking the family pick-up truck, she heads off on a journey home from California to Connecticut. Her journey allows her to meet many interesting characters (not the least is fainting goats). BBYA (nominated 2007); Booklist; SLJ

❑ Adlington, L. J. *The Diary of Pelly D*. (2005) Greenwillow. (0060766158). 288 pgs. A fictionalized tale of Toni V who finds Pelly D.'s diary while working on a demolition crew after the war. As he reads the diary he begins to question his own set of beliefs. A thoughtful examination of his life as he knew it. BBYA (2006); Booklist; BCCB

❑ Adoff, Jaime. *Jimi and Me*. (2005) Hyperion/Jump at the Sun. (0786852143). 336 pgs. Keith James and his father admire Jimi Hindrix and his music. But then Keith's father is violently killed and grief consumes Keith. He and his mother are left in near-poverty and then grief turns to rage when Keith discovers why his father left his family little money— he had another family and another Jimi. Verse novel. John Steptoe Award for New Talent. BBYA (nominated 2007)

Connections—Jimi Hendrix
Jimi Hendrix's use of the electric guitar forever changed the landscape of music. He was born on November 27, 1942 and started playing on a $5 guitar that his father bought for him when he was 16 (the same year his mother died). By the following year he was playing on an electric guitar and after a short stint in the army, he devoted his life to making a mark in the music world. He died of suffocation on September 18, 1970— he was just 27. More about his brief but influential life can be found at the Rock and Roll Hall of Fame (online): http://www.rockhall.com/hof/inductee.asp?id=130

❑ Akbar, Said Hyder and Burton, Susan. **Come Back to Afghanistan: A California Teenager's Story.** (2005) Bloomsbury. (1582345201). 336 pgs. Three summers in Afghanistan helping to rebuild the country— Hyder, a California teen and his father. Non-fiction; BBYA2006-Top10; BBYA (2006); SLJ

Book Note

Come Back to Afghanistan: A California Teenager's Story is based on the meticulous notes and journal entries made during three trips to his father's homeland. His father, Fazel Akbar, was Afghan President Hamid Karzai's former spokesman and former governor of Kunar province. A real-life story chronicled on CNN and in several international news stories. Read the back story behind this book on the Asia Times Online book review page: "Rebuilding Pangs" a review by Sreeram Chaulia at http://www.atimes.com/atimes/South_Asia/HB04Df02.html

❑ Alexander, Robert. **Rasputin's Daughter.** (2006) Penguin Group USA/Viking. (0670034681). 320 pgs. Was Rasputin a saint or sinner? This is a smoothly written fictional account of Rasputin's last week of life and of the demise of the Romanov Dynasty of Russia. Marie, Rasputin's daughter, shares a new view of her father—for good or bad. BBYA (nominated 2007)

❑ Anderson, Laurie Halse. **Prom.** (2005) Viking. (0670059749) 224 pgs. Ashley Hannigan doesn't much care about her senior prom, but her best friend Natalia is very much involved. Natalia is head of the committee planning the prom. When the faculty advisor takes the funds Natalia is faced with a problem: creating a prom with no funds. A rite-of-passage event. BCCB; Booklist; Kirkus; Kliatt

Author Note

Laurie Halse Anderson's website http://www.writerlady.com. Look for discussion guide questions and a sample from the first chapter of **Prom.**

❑ Aronson, Marc. **The Real Revolution: The Global Story of the American Revolution.** (2005) Clarion. (0618181792). 240 pgs. A portrait of how our nation came to be; new facts and insights into the people and events. New names to associate: Tom Paine in America and Robert Clive in India. Booklist; BCCB; SLJ; SLJ Best Books

❑ Balliett, Blue. **Wright 3.** (2006) Illustrated by Brett Helquist. Scholastic. (0439693675). 318 pgs. Petra Andalee and Calder Pillary are back, this time with their friend Tommy. The three friends find themselves in the midst of solving a mystery that concerns the Robie House designed by Frank Lloyd Wright in 1909. Together they piece together the puzzle that will help save the building. Companion title to **Chasing Vermeer** (2004).

Connections

For a quick look at the history behind the Romanov Dynasty of Russia (1631-1917) visit the e-museum at Minnesota State University, Mankato http://www.mnsu.edu/emuseum/history/russia/romanov.html. Nicholas II, the last Romanov Tsar was forced to abdicate on March 15, 1917, partially as a result of the influence Rasputin had on the government. Nicholas II and his entire family were executed on July 17, 1918. Read "Rasputin, the Monk Who Brought Down a Dynasty" by Jennifer Brainard at the HistoryWiz site: http://www.historywiz.com/historymakers/rasputin.htm

❑ Barnard, Bryn. *Outbreak: Plagues That Changed History*. (2005) Crown. (0375829865). 47 pgs. The major diseases of the world are explored, along with the diseases' effect on history and the culture. Well-researched volume includes illustrations and maps that show the geographical route that the infections traveled. VOYA Non-fiction

❑ Bartoletti, Susan Campbell. *Hitler Youth: Growing Up in Hitler's Shadow*. (2005) Scholastic. Illustrated with photographs. (0439353793). 176 pgs. It was Adolf Hitler's goal to use the young people of his nation to accomplish his evil master plan for global domination. Nonfiction BBYA2006-Top10 BBYA (2006); Booklist; Horn Book; Kirkus; PW; SLJ; VOYA Non-fiction

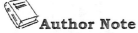

Author Note

Find out about the emergence of Susan Campbell Bartoletti as a writer by visiting her website at http://www.scbartoletti.com/

❑ Bechard, Margaret. *Spacer and Rat*. (2005) Roaring Brook/Deborah Brodie. (1596430583). 192 pgs. Jack has spent his whole life in space and is now leaving to go to Liberty when he runs into an Earthie, Kit, who ends up endangering Jack's plans and his life. A "rat" is someone like an Earthie who is deemed not to contribute to society in general. Bechard literary allusions to science-fiction writers and snappy space slang. BBYA (2006)

❑ Belth, Alex. *Stepping Up: The Story of Curt Flood and His Fight for Baseball Players' Rights*. (2006) Persea. (0892553219). 2224 pgs. This book makes the case for Curt Flood and his immeasurable influence on today's game of baseball. Non-fiction; BBYA (nominated 2007).

Connections—Curt Flood and Baseball Rights

The man who gave up his career to protest injustice in the Big Leagues died of throat cancer two days after his 59th birthday. Curt Flood's baseball career was shortened by his efforts to right an injustice, but his influence lives on. More information at the Baseball Reliquary, Inc. site http://www.baseballreliquary.org/flood.htm

---

❑ Belton, Sandra. *Store-Bought Baby*. (2006) HarperCollins/Greenwillow. (0060850868). 256 pgs. Leah often felt she was a disappointment to her mother, and that her adopted older brother, Luce, was a favored child. But Luce dies in a car-accident and Leah is left to ponder the mysteries of Luce's life. Her search for answers leads her to understand much about "real" families. BBYA (nominated 2007)

❑ Benanav, Michael. *Men of Salt: Crossing the Sahara on the Caravan of White Gold*. (2006) Globe Pequot/Lyons. (1592287727). 256 pgs. Details Benanav's journey—forty days north on a camel caravan from the legendary city of Timbuktu in Mali to the remote salt-mining outpost of Taoudenni to obtain salt, a substance worth more than its weight in gold. The author experiences one of the last caravans before the centuries old tradition gave way to trucks that will soon compete for the business. Non-fiction; BBYA (nominated 2007); PW

Connections—The Salt Mines of Taoudenni
National Public Radio puts the vanishing culture in perspective in a four part radio expedition recounted in "On the Edge, Timbuktu Radio Expeditions: Researcher Heads to Sahara to Study Vanishing Cultures" by Alex Chadwick. http://www.npr.org/templates/story/story.php?storyId=1275887

❏ Black, Holly. ***Valiant: A Modern Tale of Faerie***. (2005) Simon & Schuster. (0689868227). 320 pgs. Val runs away to the bowels of New York City where she meets the trolls in the "faerie world" and a homeless trio who introduces her to subway squatting and dumpster diving. She is exposed to the Faerie's dangerous drug "Never." When a murder plot unfolds Val's admiration for Ravus, the troll accused of murder, it makes her come to terms with her life in order to investigate and find the real murderer. Earthy and sometimes raunchy language in an urban-gothic setting may deter some readers and attract others. BBYA (2006)

📖 **Author Note**
Not only is Holly Black a writer of dark and edgy fiction, her own life borders on the dark and edgy. She met her future husband, Theo Black at a Dungeons & Dragons event. Together they moved to Philadelphia to attend college and married in 1999. After college, she had a job at the D8 gaming magazine. It was during this time that she wrote her first successful novel, *Tithe: A Modern Faerie Tale* and later collaborated with fellow D8 employee, Tony DiTerlizzi. Together they wrote the five book series, Spiderwick Chronicles. Learn more about Holly Black online at http://www.hollyblack.com

---

❏ Blackwood, Gary. ***Second Sight.*** (2005) Dutton. (0525474811). 288 pgs. An alternate history that takes us to the assassination of Abraham Lincoln. Father and son Nicolas and Joseph Ehrlich are mind readers who make sense of a secret coded alphabet. They become acquainted with Cassandra Quinn. Together they foresee the actions of John Wilkes Booth and set out to prevent the disaster. Many historical details interspersed with fictional characters who turn history around. BCCB, Kirkus

---

Connections—More Reading
Alternative history involves revisiting a period of history in which one or more past events is changed and the subsequent effects on history are described. The description may determine the entire plot of a novel or may provide the backdrop for a short story or a short episode in a longer piece of writing. Two popular themes in alternative histories surround the questions, "What if the Nazis won World War II?" and "What if the Confederacy won the American Civil War?" For a list of over 2700 alternative history documents visit Uchronia: The Alternative History List (online) http://www.uchronia.net/

❏ Bloor, Edward. ***London Calling***. (2006) Random House/Knopf. (0375836357). A time travel adventure that takes Martin back to London during the 1941 Blitz. BBYA (nominated 2007)

❏ Blumenthal, Karen. ***Let Me Play: The Story of Title IX: The Law That Changed the Future of Girls in America.*** (2005) Simon & Schuster/Atheneum. Illustrated. (0689859570). 180 pgs. Until 1972, females were not given opportunities in the sports world: college/school funds were unequally distributed for male/female sports. Title IX changed the dynamics of sports in America. Non-fiction; BBYA (2006); SLJ

❑ Bolden, Tonya. *Maritcha: A Nineteenth Century American Girl*. (2005) Abrams. Illustrated. (0810950456). 48 pgs. A free slave in the "free North" must still struggle to live a normal life. Maritcha Lyons, born of a free African American family in New York in 1843, managed to live an amazing life peppered with influence from events in American history. Acquainted with many who were important figures in the abolitionist movement Maritcha's story provides a unique look at free Blacks in the mid-nineteenth century. Non-fiction; BBYA (2006); Booklist

❑ Bondoux, Anne-Laure. *The Killer's Tears*. (2006) Random House/Delacorte. (0385732937). 176 pgs. A vagrant criminal, Angel Allegria kills young Paolo's parents in the opening scene. But sparing Paolo's life sets up Angel to take over the house and the life within it. A wealthy traveler soon joins the group and he and Angel find themselves vying to be a father figure to Paolo. Eventually all three are drawn back into the mainstream of society where society's morality clashes with reality as it exists for the trio. Set in a remote area of Chili. French Prix Sorcieres Winner; BBYA (nominated 2007); Booklist; BCCB; SLJ

❑ Boyne, John. *The Boy in the Striped Pajamas: A Fable*. (2006) Random House/David Fickling. (0385751060). 224 pgs. A Holocaust tale from the viewpoint of a nine-year-old boy whose father is a commandant. Bruno makes friends with a same aged boy, Shmuel, from Krakow. Each day they meet on separate sides of the fence. BBYA (nominated 2007)

📖 More stories from Poland
Anita Lobel, a popular author/illustrator of children's books was a child of the Holocaust and spent more than five years fleeing from the Nazis in her Polish homeland. Read the true story of her flight in *No Pretty Pictures* (Greenwillow, 1998). Another very interesting story that features the true ingenuity of the children during the Holocaust years in Poland is told in a single incident picture book, *The Cats in Krasinski Square* by Karen Hesse, illustrated by Wendy Watson (Scholastic, 2004). Jerry Spinelli wrote a novel set in Poland during the Holocaust period: *Milkweed* (Knopf, 2003) tells the story of an abandoned child in the Ghetto of Warsaw.

❑ Bradley, Alex. *24 Girls in 7 Days*. (2005) Dutton. (0525473696) 256 pgs. Jack, a high school senior finds himself in a crazy social situation: he does not have a date for prom. But his friends Percy and Natalie take the matter into their own hands and put a classified ad in the school paper. Now he has 24 girls and must make a decision in 7 days.

❑ Brashares, Ann. *Girls in Pants: The Third Summer of the Sisterhood*. (2005) Delacorte. (0385729359). 352 pgs. The third volume of this popular series (*Sisterhood of the Traveling Pants* and *The Second Summer of the Sisterhood*) is cited as being inspiring and hilarious. The four friends are spending their last summer together before heading off to colleges in four different cities. BCCB; Booklist; Kliatt

The Movie

Amber Tamblyn, America Ferrera, Blake Lively and Alexis Bledel star as the four friends. Carmen, Bridget, Lena, and Tibby are ready to embark on life after high school and the shared pair of pants help to take them on the journey. Produced by Warner Brothers, the movie is now available on DVD and presents an excellent opportunity to compare the series with the depiction on screen. For more information go to the movie's official site at: http://sisterhoodofthetravelingpants.warnerbros.com/

❑ Bray, Libba. **Rebel Angels**. (2005) Delacorte. (0385730292). 560 pgs. A fantasy that has brought magic to all through Gemma's act of breaking the runes. Now will she have the strength to give the magic back to its rightful possessors, the Order? Sequel to *A Great and Terrible Beauty* (2003). BBYA (2006)

❑ Brooks, Kevin. **Candy.** (2005) Chicken House. (0439683270). 368 pgs. Joe's life is rather mundane until he meets Candy. As he gets closer to Candy, he also gets closer to her world, a world filled with drugs and violent confrontations. His life turns to one of dark desperation. Danger seems to be at every turn. PW

Author Note

Making his debut as an author with **Martyn Pig** (2002) Brooks' first novel was highly acclaimed. It won the 2003 Branford Boase Award and was on the Carnegie Medal short list. That book was followed by **Lucas: A Story of Love** (2003) and **Kissing the Rain** (2004). His popularity continues and he publishes a book each year. For background information about Kevin Brooks go to http://books.scholastic.com/teachers/ and search for "Kevin Brooks" to locate his page on the "Authors and Books" site.

❑ Brooks, Kevin. **The Road of the Dead.** (2006) Scholastic/Chicken House. (0439786231). 352 pgs. Ruben can see things that others can not, and so he knows when his sister is raped and murdered in the moors of Dartmoor. Ruben also sees the trouble his older brother, Cole, is about to cause and get into when he goes to Dartmoor to discover the truth behind their sister's brutal murder. A gripping tale with scenes of brutal, vivid violence but never gratuitous. BBYA (nominated 2007)

❑ Bruchac, Joseph. **Code Talker: A Novel About the Navajo Marines of World War Two**. (2005) Dial. (0803729219). 240 pgs. A fictionalized account of the Navajo's role in World War II as code talkers using an unbreakable code to relay messages. Main protagonist is Ned Begay who has spent years in white-run boarding schools. Nonfiction collaborative book: **Navajo Code Talkers** by Nate Aaseng (Walker, 2004, pb; 0802775896) BBYA (2006); BCCB; Booklist; Kirkus

**Author Note**

Don't miss Joseph Bruchac's **Hidden Roots** (2004). Learn more about the author and his books (online) at http://www.josephbruchac.com

❑ Bruchac, Joseph. **Wabi: A Hero's Tale.** (2006) Dial. (0803730985). 2008 pgs. A fantasy tale that includes elements of romance, adventure, and folklore. Wabi has very pale feathers, has the ability to change forms, and has a very wise grandmother owl. When Wabi falls in love with Dojihla, a human Abenaki girl, he decides to shift to a human form, but he still thinks and acts like an owl. When his true identity is revealed he leaves the village. Wabi finds a wolf companion and discovers ways to protect his environment and Dojihla's people. Kirkus; SLJ

❑ Brugman, Alyssa. *Being Bindy*. (2006) Delacorte. (0385732945). 208 pgs. This should be the best time of her life, but eighth grade is pure torture. Belinda's best friend is now an ex-best friend as she has found someone more mature to hang out with. Her friend's new group smoke pot, dress to risqué, and are just plain mean. Then her father begins to date her ex-friend's mother. Could things be worse? Well, yes, at least in Belinda's eyes. A "finding self" theme from Australia. SLJ; BBYA (nominated 2007)

❑ Buckhanon, Kalisha. *Upstate*. (2005) St. Martin's. (0312332688). 256 pgs. Nine years of love letters between Natasha and Antonio. Antonio is in prison for his father's murder. Natasha is left behind in Harlem. While Antonio struggles to survive, Natasha struggles to make a life without her first love. www.kalisha.com BBYA2006-Top10, BBYA (2006)

❑ Budhos, Marina. *Ask Me No Questions*. (2006) Simon & Schuster/Atheneum/Ginee Soe. (1416903518). 176 pgs. After 9/11 a Bangladesh family, who has lived illegally for years in New York City, sense the immigration laws tightening, so they attempt to flee to Canada. When their father is detained at the Canadian border, teenage sisters Nadira and Aisha are sent back to Queens, NY to try to live "normal" lives while keeping their illegal status as secret as possible. But when Aisha has a breakdown, it is up to Nadira to gather the documentation that might prevent the family's deportation. BBYA (nominated 2007); Booklist; BCCB; Horn Book

❑ Burton, Rebecca. *Leaving Jetty Road*. (2006) Random House/Alfred A. Knopf. (037593488X). 256 pgs. Chronicles the final year of school for three friends in South Australia. Through alternating chapters, Nat and Sofia detail their decision to become vegetarians and where it takes them. Initially it takes Nat to a part-time job at the Wild Carrot Café and a first love; Sofia a serious relationship; and for Lise a struggle with anorexia. Each girl seeks to control her own life but finds that their options are taking them further and further from one another. BBYA (nominated 2007)

> **Book Note: Voice**
> One of many books written in alternating voices. Consider correlating this novel with writing instruction focusing on the Six Traits of Writing® at http://www.nwrel.org/assessment/about.php?odelay=1&d=1

❑ Caletti, Deb. *Wild Roses*. (2005) Simon & Schuster. (0689867662). 304 pgs. Everyone thinks her world-renowned step-father, Dino Cavalli, is wonderful—a wonderful violinist and a wonderful composer. But to 17-year-old Cassie Morgan he is a dangerous self-centered bully. How to cope when the world sees him differently? Coping with mental illness, a forbidden love, and the realization that there is a relationship between passion and insanity. BCCB; SLJ

❑ Caputo, Philip. *10,000 Days of Thunder: A History of the Vietnam War.* (2005) Simon & Schuster/Atheneum/Byron Preiss, (0689862318). 128 pgs. A Vietnam Vet examines the causes and repercussions of the Vietnam War. Many photographs and maps help readers understand the well-written text. Non-fiction; BBYA (nominated 2007); BCCB; SLJ; PW; VOYA Non-fiction

- Castellucci, Cecil. *Boy Proof*. (2005) Candlewick. (0763623334). 208 pgs. Victoria Denton is too bright and too tough to attract any interest from the boys or any friends in the high school. Renaming herself for her favorite character, Egg, from a science fiction movie, she dresses in the character's trademark white cloak. But then Max arrives. BBYA (2006)

- Cheney, Annie. *Body Brokers: Inside America's Underground Trade in Human Remains.* (2006) Random House/Broadway. (0767917332). 240 pgs. Unscrupulous undertakers work with body brokers to sell body parts for high prices, often without the consent of the family. Cheney presents compelling evidence to expose the profiteering that accompanies the trade. Non-fiction; BBYA (nominated 2007); Booklist

- Clee, Paul. *Before Hollywood: From Shadow Play to the Silver Screen.*.(2005) Clarion. (0618445331). 2224 pgs. The history of movies and movie making including inventions, animation, and special effects. Non-fiction; BCCB; Kirkus

- Coburn, Jake. *LoveSick*. (2005) Dutton. (0525473831). 240 pgs. A drunk driver cripples Ted and causes him to lose his basketball scholarship. He might be able to attend college if he is willing to spy on a Manhattan princess. Romance and an eating disorder served up with humor and surprises. BBYA (2006)

- Cohn, Rachel and David Levithan. *Nick and Norah's Infinite Playlist*. (2006) Random House/Alfred A. Knopf. (0375835318). 192 pgs. In alternating chapters, Norah and Nick talk of their romance, their emotions, and connections to the New York club scene. Norah has a "potty mouth." Many insightful moments and a fast-paced narrative that will entice reluctant readers. BBYA (nominated 2007); Kirkus

- Cole, Sheila. *To Be Young in America: Growing Up with the Country, 1776-1940.* (2005) Little, Brown. (031151963). 146 pgs. A collection of chapters examining many phases of life in America from love to war. Many illustrations, photos, and a collage of life from the past. VOYA Non-fiction

- Cooney, Caroline B. *Hit the Road.* (2006) Delacorte. (0385729448). 192 pgs. Brit has had her driver's license just 11 days before her parents leave for a vacation and decide to leave Brit in the capable hands of her grandmother for two weeks. But Nannie has other ideas. She wants to travel across three states to pick up her college roommates and go to their college's 65th reunion—most likely the last one they will attend. Brit thinks the trip is for Grandma but she gains much from it as well. Booklist

- Cornish, D. M. *Monster Blood Tattoo: Foundling*. (2006) Penguin Group USA/Putnam. (039924638X). 404 pgs. A world of fantasy features Rossamünd Bookchild, an orphan, who sets off to slay the monsters of the Half-Continent and a Georgian-esque society. Adventure, colorful characters, and a transition from boy to man. Maps, diagrams, and character portraits. BBYA (nominated 2007)

- Couloumbis, Audrey. *Summer's End.* (2005) Putnam. (0399235558). 192 pgs. When 13-year-old Grace's older brother, Colin, is turned out of the house after burning his draft card, she seeks refuge at her grandparents' farm to avoid her parents' arguments. The Vietnam War is affecting the entire family and ideological differences abound. This book will stimulate discussions on the merits (or demerits) of war and the importance of family. Booklist; BCCB

❑ Creech, Sharon. **Replay**. (2005) Joanna Cotler. (0060540192). 240 pgs. As the middle child, Leonardo (or Leo) is often called "Sardine" because he is sandwiched between his two siblings. He has dreams for being a dancer, a writer, and an athlete. One day, in the family's attic, Leo finds his father's journal and discovers his father had the same aspirations as a teenager. He also finds something else—a family photo that shows an unfamiliar girl. Could that girl be the Aunt Rosaria that no one speaks of? How can he get his father to speak of the memories too difficult to let go of? A drama, in which Leo is given a part, plays a pivotal role in the parallel look at the situation in Leo's family. The entire play "Rumpopo's Porch" is included at the end of the book.

❑ Davis, Sampson, George Jenkins, and Rameck Hunt. **We Beat the Street: How a Friendship Pact Led to Success**. (2005) Dutton. (0525474072). 194 pgs. Three young men, three friends, one pact. Three young black men grew up in the tough streets of New Jersey, but with luck, perseverance, and their friendship they rose above their circumstances to become doctors and are now sharing their stories in the hope of inspiring other young people to strive for their goals. VOYA Non-fiction

❑ Davidson, Dana. **Played**. (2005) Hyperion/Jump at the Sun. (0786836903). 240 pgs. Ian's initiation into an elite high school fraternity involves seducing one of the plainest girls in school and having sex with her. When his exploits are accidentally revealed to the whole school, he must find a way to make Kylie trust him again, as he has fallen in love. Kylie has true friends and is happy, while it is clear that Ian has sacrificed his integrity to have "friends" and he is far from happy. BBYA (nominated 2007)

❑ de la Peña, Matt. **Ball Don't Lie**. (2005) Delacorte. (0385732325). 288 pgs. Efforts to pull himself from poverty, life with a prostitute mother, and escape from foster care and the streets is a struggle but Sticky must. He feels that he has been born to play ball. A skinny white teen is determined to succeed, to get that college scholarship, and to leave his past behind. An unforgettable, distinctly male voice. BBYA (2006); BCCB; SLJ

❑ Deem, James M. **Bodies From the Ash: Life and Death in Ancient Pompeii**. (2005) Houghton Mifflin. Illustrated. (0618473084). 48 pgs. A quick read focusing on the eruption of Vesuvius that destroyed Pompeii in AD 79. Non-fiction; Science Books; BBYA (2006); SLJ; VOYA Non-fiction

❑ Delisle, Guy. **Pyongyang: A Journey in North Korea**. (2005) Drawn and Quarterly. Illustrated (1896597890). 184 pgs. When an animation company in communist North Korea is awarded an outsourcing contract for an animation project, a French Canadian, Guy Delisle, is sent to oversee the project. This is a simple and funny graphic novel. Non-fiction; BBYA (2006)

❑ Dendy, Leslie and Mel Boring. **Guinea Pig Scientists: Bold Self-Experimenters in Science and Medicine**. (2005) Holt. Illustrated. (0805073167). Ten dedicated and determined scientists used themselves as subjects for experiments that each felt was crucial to the success of their exploration. Non-fiction; BBYA (2006); Science Books; SLJ; Booklist

Author Note

The two authors worked on this book for over a decade. Boring lived in Iowa during much of that time and Dendy was a resident of New Mexico. Their work was done electronically and prior to the publication of the book the authors had not met in person. For more information about Boring check out (online) http://www.authorsillustrators.com/boring/bio.htm. Find out more about the book and Madame Curie, one of the scientist's featured from the Children's Literature site at http://www.childrenslit.com/ft_curie.html

❑ Dessen, Sarah. *Just Listen*. (2006) Penguin Group USA/Viking. (0670061050). 384 pgs. After Annabel Greene is caught with her best friend Sophie's boyfriend, her cool friends turn their backs on her. No one would believe that the situation was attempted rape. With the loss of her cool friends and her family in shambles over her sister's eating disorder, Annabel is dreading the beginning of her junior year. A school loner, Owen, who has his own issues to face, helps her realize the danger in holding in her emotions and encouraging her to speak out. Pair this with Laura Halse Anderson's *Speak* (1999). BBYA (nominated 2007)

❑ Dorfman, Joaquin. *Playing it Cool*. (2006) Random House. (0375836411). 352 pgs. Sebastian Montero is known as the town's problem solver—he can arrange for anything to happen. But when his friend, Jeremy, asks for help finding his biological dad, Sebastian finds himself in over his head. There's more to the story of Jeremy's father, Dromio, than what is on the surface. BBYA (nominated 2007); SLJ

❑ Draper, Sharon. *Copper Sun*. (2006) Simon & Schuster/Atheneum (0689821816). 320 pgs. Amari is living in a calm peaceful Ashanti village until slave traders raid the village, kill her parents, take her away in shackles, and put her on a slave ship bound for America. Raped repeatedly onboard ship and at the slave auction, she is bought by a rice plantation owner for his 16-year-old son's sexual pleasure. Amari meets a white indentured servant, Polly, and both of them suffer the wrath of Mr. Derby. They plot an escape to the freedom of Fort Mose, a Spanish colony in Florida. Befriended by the doctor who provides the opportunity for their flight and an Irish woman who gives them a horse and buggy, the two flee their inhuman state. Readers will learn much about the state of slavery, indentured servitude, and 18th century slave sanctuaries. BBYA (nominated 2007); Booklist; SLJ; BCCB

❑ Duble, Kathleen Benner. *The Sacrifice*. (2005) Simon & Schuster/Margaret K. McElderry. (0689876505). 224 pgs. This is ten-year-old Abigail's story of being accused of witchcraft in 1692 in Andover, Massachusetts. Are she and her older sister agents of the devil? And what will become of the wide-spread accusations? Duble's own ancestors' family share part of this story. Pair with Arthur Miller's *The Crucible*; Ellen Levine's *Catch a Tiger by the Toe* (2005); and Marc Aronson's informational account, *Witch-Hunt* (2003). BBYA (nominated 2007); Booklist

❑ Eisner, Will. *The Plot: The Secret Story of the Protocols of the Elders of Zion*. (2005) W.W. Norton. Illustrated. (0-393-06045-4). 148 pgs. The Protocol document was a fraud (and historical treatise) but has been oft quoted by Klansmen, Hitler, and other defamation groups to further their cause. Graphic Non-fiction; BBYA (2006)

❑ Farrell, Jeanette. *Invisible Allies: Microbes That Shape Our Lives.* (2005) Farrar. (0374336083). 176 pgs. Microbes as they positively affect our lives; follows a cheese sandwich and a chocolate bar and examines the microbes involved from beginning to end. Non-fiction; BBYA (2006); Booklist; BCCB; Horn Book; SLJ

❑ Ferguson, Alane. *Angel of Death: Forensic Mystery II.* (2006) Penguin Group USA/Viking/Sleuth. (0670060550). 256 pgs. Cameryn continues as her father's assistant and finds herself in the middle of a bizarre situation when the most popular student in school finds the gruesome corpse of their English teacher in his bed. Cameryn has a secret of her own: her long-ago vanished mother is back in her life.. Is Cameryn too self-occupied to solve the murder of the English teacher in time to prevent more tragedy?

📖**Author Note**

Alane Ferguson's first novel, *Show Me the Evidence* (Bradbury, 1989) brought her quickly into the realm of writing for young adults when her book won an Edgar Award. Since then she has written mover 25 additional novels, some with her mother Gloria Skurzynski. http://www.alaneferguson.com

---

❑ Ferguson, Alane. *The Christopher Killer: Forensic Mystery 1.* (2006) Penguin Group USA/Viking/Sleuth. (0670060089). 288 pgs. Fascinated with forensic science, 17-year-old Cameryn convinces her dad, a coroner, to hire her as an assistant. Cameryn soon is called upon to help solve the case of a serial murderer who has just murdered one of her friends. Cameryn's efforts put her in danger of becoming victim number 5. A compelling mystery-thriller. BBYA (nominated 2007)

❑ Fisher, Catherine. **Darkhenge**. (2006) HarperCollins/Greenwillow. (0060785829). 352 pgs. Drawing on Celtic mythology, this literary tale of fantasy explores mystery and dark magic. Rob manages to land a job at an archaeological dig. Sensing that the henge might have something to do with his sister's coma, Rob eventually enters the world of Anwyn and discovers that his sister's spirit has withdrawn because of anger with her brother. The heavy dose of folkloric elements and changing perspectives will make this book one for able readers. BBYA (nominated 2007)

❑ Fisher, Catherine. *Day of the Scarab: Book Three of the Oracle Prophecies*. (2006) Greenwillow. (0060571632). 416 pgs. General Argelin has seized control. Archon must find the power that is hidden in the sign of the Scarab and how will Mirany and the Archon find a journey through the Nine Gateways into death and back? Horn Book; Kirkus

❑ Flake, Sharon G. *Bang!* (2005) Hyperion/Jump at the Sun. (0786818441). 304 pgs. Mann's father feels he lost one son because of his protectiveness. Determined it won't happen again, he insists Mann learn his own lessons. He abandons Mann and a friend in the wilderness to survive on their own. When Mann makes it home, he is again turned out, this time to live on the streets. BBYA (2006)

❑ Flanagan, John. *The Burning Bridge: The Ranger's Apprentice: Book II*. (2006) Penguin Group USA/Philomel. (0399244557). 256 pgs. The war against the evil Morgarath continues in this sequel to *The Ruins of Gorlan* (2005). Will and his battleschool apprentice comrades discover a nearly completed bridge that will facilitate sneak attacks into their kingdom. High adventure and down-to-earth characters. BBYA (nominated 2007)

❑ Flanagan, Timothy. ***Reconstruction: A Primary Source History of the Struggle to Unite the North and South after the Civil War.*** (2005) Rosen. (1404201777) Primary source materials dealing with the basic information and timelines for the Reconstruction period of United States history. Part of the Primary Sources in America History series. VOYA Non-fiction

❑ Fleming, Candace. ***Our Eleanor: A Scrapbook Look at Eleanor Roosevelt's Remarkable Life.*** (2005) Simon & Schuster/Atheneum Illustrated. (0689865449). 192 pgs. Another scrapbook-format biography (her first subject was Benjamin Franklin). This one is of Eleanor Roosevelt. From her childhood, through marriage and motherhood, into her public life, and years as First Lady. Artifacts of her many accomplishments as an astute politician, writer, social activist, delegate to the UN, and protectorate of those in need, are highlighted. Non-fiction; BBYA (2006); SLJ; VOYA Non-fiction

---

Colloborative Book List

Read more books about the life of Eleanor Roosevelt:

Freedman, Russell. (1994) ***Eleanor Roosevelt: A Life of Discovery.*** Clarion. Sawyer, Kem Knapp. (2006) ***Eleanor Roosevelt.*** DK Children. Don't miss Barbara Cooney's elegant, well-researched picture book biography of Eleanor Roosevelt, ***Eleanor*** (Viking, 1996)

❑ Fradin, Judith Bloom and Dennis Brindell Fradin. ***5,000 Miles to Freedom: Ellen and William Craft's Flight From Slavery.*** (2006) National Geographic. (0792278852). 96 pgs. A moving story of a slave couple who pose as a white man (Ellen) with his male servant (William) traveling north to freedom. Their plight and eventual notoriety send them further away for safety as they spend several years in England to escape the bounty hunters who come north to hunt runaway slaves. Non-fiction; BBYA (nominated 2007)

Book Note

The story of Ellen and William Craft is told by Julius Lester as one of three stories in ***This Strange New Feeling: Three Love Stories from Black History*** (Dial, 1982; 2007).

❑ Frank, E. R. ***Wrecked.*** (2005) Simon & Schuster/Atheneum. (0689873832). 256 pgs. After a car accident in which her brother's girl friend is killed and her own best friend is injured, Anna, 16, suffers from post-traumatic stress disorder. Anna's emotionally abusive father does not contribute positively to the situation. BBYA (2006)

❑ Frank, Mitch. ***Understanding the Holy Land: Answering Questions About the Israeli-Palestinian Conflict.*** (2005) Viking. Illustrated. (0670060321). 160 pgs. Through questions and answers the Israeli-Palestinian conflict is examined. Provides background for the events in the Middle East during the summer of 2006. Non-fiction; BBYA (2006); Booklist ; VOYA Non-fiction

❑ Freymann-Weyr, Garret. ***Stay with Me.*** (2006) Houghton Mifflin, (0618605711). 320 pgs. Sixteen-year-old Leila is caught in a world of adults where she struggles to find her place. Rebecca, Clare, and their mother have always been mysterious to Leila. When their mother dies, Rebecca commits suicide. Leila goes to live with Clare and searches for answers to her own complex relationships, including a mutual attraction to 31-year-old Eamon. A complicated coming-of-age tale. BBYA (nominated 2007); Booklist

❏ Gaiman, Neil. ***Anansi Boys***. (2005) HarperCollins/William Morrow. (006051518X). 352 pgs. Dark humor. Father-son and brother relationships—all characters who have a relationship with Anansi, the spiderman trickster from African folklore. BBYA (2006); PW

❏ Gallego Garcia, Laura. ***The Valley of the Wolves***. (2006) Scholastic/Arthur A. Levine. (0439585538). 336 pgs. A fast moving fantasy tale that takes place in the Great Tower in the Valley where Dana has been sent to study sorcery. She and her invisible friend Kai, who has accompanied her, find that they have become caught up in the search for the Unicorn. Defying her mentor's warnings against entering the night woods, Dana and Kai face the wolves and explore the powers she does have. BBYA (nominated 2007)

❏ Galloway, Gregory. ***As Simple as Snow***. (2005) Putnam. (0399152318). 320 pgs. When Anastasia (Anna), a High school student, disappears, the only thing left is a neatly laid out dress by a hole in the ice. BBYA (2006); ALEX

❏ Gantos, Jack. ***The Love Curse of the Rumbaugh***s. (2006) Farrar, Straus and Giroux. (0374336903). 185 pgs. Ivy is just seven years old when this dark and perverse tale in the ultra gothic style begins. Lined with allusions to incest, perverse love for one's mother, and an extreme and compulsive interest in taxidermy that might always keep her mother with her, makes this book one for older teens. Characters include identical albino twins, Abner and Adolph, who run the local pharmacy where Ivy spends many of her days. A strange book even for those who enjoy darkly comic horror tales. BBYA (nominated 2007); Kirkus; Booklist; SLJ; VOYA; Chicago Tribune

❏ Garden, Nancy. ***Endgame***. (2006) Harcourt. (0152054162). 287 pgs. Gray was hoping for a new start but the bullies at Greenford High did not take long to find him. Zorro's continuing harassment of Gray, ignored by anyone in authority, culminates with Gray bringing a gun to school after Zorro and his buddies hit and kill Gray's dog and try to force Gray and his friend Ross into a sex act in the school showers. The story unfolds through interviews with Gray in the juvenile detention center waiting for his murder trail. A shocking look at the impact of bullying and violence. BBYA (nominated 2007); SLJ; Kirkus; Booklist

❏ Geras, Adele. ***Ithaka***. (2006) Harcourt. (0152056033). 368 pgs. Playing on the theme of the *The Odyssey* and those that were left behind, Geras restructures the tale through the eyes of the servant girl, Klymene and re-imagines the events that take place while those who are left behind wait for Odysseus to return from the Trojan War. A fine companion to pair with the classic tale, just as *Troy* (2001) paired with *The Iliad*. BBYA (nominated 2007)

❏ Giblin, James Cross. ***Good Brother, Bad Brother: The Story of Edwin Booth and John Wilkes Booth***. (2005) Clarion. Illustrated. (0618096426). 254 pgs. John Wilkes Booth is remembered for assassinating President Abraham Lincoln. Edwin Booth made his mark as an actor, but after the death of Lincoln, his fame was as the brother of the man who assassinated the President. Presents a unique look at the events that lead up to John Wilkes Booth's involvement. Non-fiction; BBYA (2006); BCCB; Booklist; Kirkus; SLJ

Gideon, Melanie. *Pucker*. (2006) Penguin Group USA/Razorbill, 2006. (1595140557). 256 pgs. Thomas left the alternative world, Isaura, as a child with his widowed mother. Even though disfigured, with burns that bring others to nickname him "Pucker," he has adapted well to life in America. But now his mother is losing her life force and she implores him to return to Isaura, facing much danger in losing his own free will and complete the quest that will restore her Seerskin and restore her life force. A dangerous journey back into an alternative world. BBYA (nominated 2007)

Giles, Gail. *What Happened to Cass McBride?* (2006) Little, Brown. (0316166383). 224 pgs. When her brother commits suicide, a revengeful college student knows just who is to blame—Cass McBride. What follows is a plot that is meant to deal with Cass – snobby, rich, and popular with everyone except those who really know what she has done. Drugged, kidnapped, and buried alive—what happened to Cass McBride? BBYA (nominated 2007)

Glass, Linzi Alex. *The Year the Gypsies Came*. (2006) Henry Holt. (0805079998). 272 pgs. It is the '60s and Apartheid is strong. Emily's white South African family is in shambles. In an effort to detract attention from their crumbling family, 12-year-old Emily's parents invite a family of Gypsies to live in a mobile home on their compound. The Gypsy family brings their own problems: a brain-damaged older son, likely the result of the father's violence, and another son that becomes Emily's friend. Apartheid does not seem to resonate until Buza, Emily's family night watchman, is arrested for not having papers and Emily becomes aware of his legally enforced life-long separation from his own daughter and family. A sad book and coming-of-age novel. BBYA (nominated 2007); Kirkus

Gravelle, Karen. *The Driving Book: Everything New Drivers Need to Know But Don't Know to Ask.* (2005) Illustrated by Helen Flook. Walker. (0802789331) Not new information for veteran drivers, but this book is meant for "new " drivers and will provide them with much to think about. Covers all the normal topics (as the state driving manual does) but adds some common sense tips as well. VOYA Non-fiction; SLJ

Green, John. *Looking for Alaska*. (2005) Dutton. (0525475060). 160 pgs. Miles meets the captivating, completely over-the-edge, vivacious Alaska at an Alabama boarding school—and that is just the beginning. BBYA2006-Top10 TeensTop10 BBYA (2006); BCCB; Booklist; Kirkus; SLJ; Michael L. Printz Award 2006.

Green, John. *An Abundance of Katherines.* (2006) Dutton. (0525476881). 256 pgs. Every Katherine he has ever loved has dumped him, and now Colin, an expert at creating anagrams, thinks he'll never get himself recognized as a genius. So he and his best friend Hassan rev up their old gray Olds and head south. From Chicago they make it as far as Gutshot, Tennessee where Colin meets a girl—not a Katherine but a Lindsey. Their work together results in a mathematical theorem estimating the length of his romantic relationships and brings humor to the story that details Colin's real contribution to the world. BBYA (nominated 2007)

Griffin, Adele. *Where I Want to Be*. (2005) Putnam. (0399237836). 160 pgs. Jane and Lily have had a close but troubled relationship. Then Jane dies, and Lily is left to come to terms with what might have been. BBYA (2006); BCCB; Booklist; Kirkus

❑ Grimes, Nikki. *Dark Sons.* (2005) Hyperion/Jump at the Sun. (0786818883). 224 pgs. Verse novel. Sam, an African-American teen, must find a way to deal with his parents' divorce and his relationship with his father, his new white mom, and the baby half-brother named Sam. This plot mimics the theme of the biblical story of Ishmael, son of Abraham, and his despair of being replaced by Isaac. BBYA (2006); Booklist

❑ *Growing Up in Slavery: Stories of Young Slaves as Told By Themselves.* (2005) Edited by Yuval Taylor. Lawrence Hill. Illustrated. (1556525486). 256 pgs. Ten intense American slave narratives filled with brutality, perseverance, will power and a triumphant spirit. Primary source narratives. Introduction is informative and the author provides recommendations for further reading. Nonfiction BBYA (2006)

❑ Gruber, Michael. *The Witch's Boy.* (2005) HarperTempest. (0060761644). 384 pgs. An ugly baby boy is found in the woods by a witch who raises him as her son. While the witch is adept at magic, she is not experienced as a mother. But she finds a bear who will be the child's nursemaid and involves a djinni as Sam's tutor. Look for bits and pieces of "Little Red Riding Hood," "Hansel and Gretel," and "Rumplestiltskin." BBYA (2006); Booklist; BCCB

❑ Haab, Sherri and Michelle Haab. *Dangles and Bangles: 25 Funky Accessories to Make and Wear.* (2005) Illustrated by Barbara Pollak. Watson-Guptill. (0823000648) 96 pgs. A craft book that delivers what it advertises—instructions for 25 inexpensive and fun projects that promote creative artistry. VOYA Non-fiction

❑ Halam, Ann. *Siberia: A Novel.* (2005) Random/Wendy Lamb. (0385746504). 272 pgs. A 13-year-old girl, Sloe, is dedicated to finding a safe place for the DNA of genetically engineered lost animal species. She must find a way to smuggle the DNA through the barren wilderness past thieves and outlaws. BBYA (2006)

❑ Haney, Eric L. *Inside Delta Force: The Story of America's Elite Counterterrorist Unit.* (2006) Random House/Delacorte. (0385732511). 256 pgs. A veteran of the Delta Force provides a glimpse into the unit and its secret world. Readers get a glance at how the unit is formulated, the selection of members, and the training. An adaptation of the author's adult book with the same title (Dell, 2002). Non-fiction; BBYA (nominated 2007)

❑ Hardinge, Frances. *Fly by Night.* (2006) HarperCollins. (0060876271). 496 pgs. In a fractured, fantastical Britain with intense warring over the written word, a twelve-year-old orphan girl and her homicidal goose find adventure. BBYA (nominated 2007) SLJ

❑ Hautman, Pete. *Invisible.* (2005) Simon & Schuster. (0689868006). 160 pgs. His teachers think he is highly disturbed. His parents do too. 17-year-old Doug's classmates view him as creepy. It is only Andy who understands him, and together they have deep secrets. BBYA (2006); BCCB; Horn Book; PW; SLJ

❑ Hautman, Pete. *Rash.* (2006) Simon & Schuster. ((068972682). The world as it might be in 2076 when anyone is punished for the infraction of being angry, fat, verbally abusing, or engage unsafe activity. Major amounts of safety equipment are required for any sport. Over 24% of the country's population is incarcerated and doing much of the country's labor. A satirical sports novel that has 16-year-old Bo Marsten being recruited for the (illegal) prison football team. Much to ponder. BBYA (nominated 2007)

❑ Hearn, Julie. *The Minister's Daughter*. (2005) Simon & Schuster/Atheneum. (0689876904). 272 pgs. The fate of Nell and the minister's daughters (Grace and Patience) are threatened when Grace accuses Nell and her grandmother of witchcraft. BBYA (2006)

❑ Hiaasen, Carl. *Flush*. (2005) Knopf. (0375921826). 272 pgs. When Noah's father gets arrested for sinking the Coral Queen casino boat in retaliation for the boat's flagrant dumping of raw sewage into the waters of the Florida Keys. Noah (and the community) gets involved and vows to finish the job. BBYA (2006)

❑ Hobbs, Will. *Crossing the Wire*. (2006) HarperCollins. (0060741384). 224 pgs. Economic factors and the disappearing market for corn in his Mexican village causes Victor (15) to make the desperate decision to leave his mother and siblings behind and attempt to cross the border in the hopes of finding a job to support his family. All the dangers of crossing and the rough terrain will not deter his determination to keep his family from starvation. Another story of the cross from Mexico to the U.S. is Ann Jaramillos' *La Linea* (Roaring Brook, 2006). BBYA (nominated 2007)

❑ Hoffman, Alice. *Incantation.* (2006) Little, Brown. (0316010197). 176 pgs. Estrella's Spanish Jewish family's double life began at a time when the alternative to a conversion to Christianity was to risk everything. Estrella discovers that her family secretly follows the ancient practices of kabbalah. The betrayal of a friend brings her to a dangerous confrontation with evil. BBYA (nominated 2007)

❑ Hokenson, Terry. *The Winter Road*. (2006) Front Street. (1932425454). 175 pgs. Learning to fly an airplane is Willa's determined effort to gain her father's approval and somehow take the place of her older brother who has died. She has learned to fly her Uncle Jordy's Cessna 185, but one day when she is scheduled to pick-up her mother, a visiting nurse, she finds her uncle drunk and she makes the hasty decision to fly the plane solo. A storm and crash-landing begins her 18-day fight for survival. Compare with Gary Paulsen's *The Hatchet* (Atheneum/Richard Jackson, 2000 reissue). BBYA (nominated 2007)

❑ Holub, Josef. *An Innocent Soldier*. (2005) Translated by Michael Hofmann. Scholastic/Arthur A. Levine. (0439627710). 240 pgs. Adam, a farm-hand who is sent to Napoleon's army in place of the farmer's son, joins the march on Russia in 1811. His eventual friendship with a well-born lieutenant is solidified as each helps the other survive the slow walk to Moscow and the retreat home. BBYA (2006)

❑ Hopkinson, Deborah. *Up before Daybreak: Cotton and People in America.* (2006) Scholastic Nonfiction. (0439639018). 128 pgs. From the cotton fields before the Civil War when King Cotton reigned to the present, Deborah Hopkinson recounts the history of the industry using many oral histories and archival photographs. Non-fiction; BBYA (nominated 2007); Kirkus; Booklist, SLJ

❑ Houston, Julian. *New Boy*. (2005) Houghton Mifflin. (0618432531). 288 pgs. A native of Virginia, fifteen-year-old Rob Garrett is to become the first black student at an exclusive Connecticut boarding school. Touched by the ostracism of Vinnie, a New York-Italian who suffers from acne and who does not fit in with his elitist classmates and his chance meeting with Malcolm X in Harlem, with his outspoken separatist attitude that preaches against association with whites and Jews. Rob realizes that racism comes in many forms. BBYA (nominated 2007); Booklist; PW

❑ Hubner, John. *Last Chance in Texas: The Redemption of Criminal Youth.* (2005) Random House. (0375508090). 304 pgs. This redemption effort claims a 90% success rate with only 10% of the capital offenders re-offending after a 3 year probation (according to a 2004 study). This account examines in detail the stories of Elena and Ronnie—two young offenders. Those who do not cooperate are sent to complete their sentences (sometimes 25–40 years) in the state penitentiary. Non-fiction; BBYA (nominated 2007); PW

❑ Hughes, Lynne B. *You Are Not Alone: Teens Talk About Life After the Loss of a Parent.* (2005) Scholastic. (0439585902) 192 pgs. Teens offer their own testimonials and advice about dealing with the death of a parent or parents. The author runs a camp for grieving children and teens. VOYA Non-fiction

❑ Hunt, Scott, illustrator. *Twice Told: Original Stories Inspired by Original Artwork.* (2006) Penguin Group USA/Dutton. (0525468188). 272 pgs. Nine charcoal drawings—two stories for each drawing: Nancy Werlin; Alex Flinn; Audrey Couloumbis; John Green; M.T. Anderson; William Sleator; Sarah Dessen; Ellen Wittlinger; Gene Brewer; Bruce Coville; Ron Koertge; Adèle Geras; Jan Marino; Marilyn Singer; Margaret Peterson Haddix; Jaime Adoff; Neal Shusterman; David Lubar. BBYA (nominated 2007); Booklist

❑ Hyde, Catherine Ryan. *Becoming Chloe.* (2006) Random House/Alfred A. Knopf. (0375832580). 224 pgs. Seventeen-year-old Jordan has been abused by his father for being gay, is homeless and out on the streets. Risking his life to rescue 18-year-old Chloe from a gang rape, the two lonely outcasts form a sibling-like bond that strengthens as they struggle, together, to survive on the streets of New York City. The two find a beat-up pickup truck and leave the city behind and hope for a new life. Survival and a healing journey to Niagara Falls and the Big Sur—and a family they have created. BBYA (nominated 2007); Kirkus; BCCB; PW

❑ Ingram, Scott. *Want Fries with That? Obesity and the Supersizing of America.* (2005) Franklin Watts. (0531167569) 128 pgs. A well-researched look at the real cost of the food we eat. Facts, statistics, and anecdotes that will cause readers to think about the food we eat. VOYA Non-fiction

❑ Jackson, Donna M. *ER Vets: Life in an Animal Emergency Room.* (2005) Houghton Mifflin. (0618436634) 88 pgs. Many photographs document treatments for a variety of animals. VOYA Non-fiction

❑ Jacobson, Jennifer Richard. *Stained.* (2005) Simon & Schuster/Atheneum. (068986745X). 208 pgs. Told from Jocelyn's perspective, this novel examines first love (Jocelyn and Benny) and their friend Gabe's emotional life after he succumbs to Father Warren's demands. BBYA (2006); Horn Book; Kirkus; PW

❑ Jaramillo, Ann. *La Linea.* (2006) Roaring Brook/Deborah Brodie. (1596431547). 144 pgs. Miguel's parents are in the United States and at 15 he has waited for years to join them. When his father sends him the money to leave Mexico, he sets off on the journey to the North—a dangerous and treacherous journey. Pair with Will Hobbs's *Crossing Wire* (2006). BBYA (nominated 2007); Booklist

❑ Jenkins, A. M. *Beating Heart: A Ghost Story.* (2006) HarperCollins/HarperTempest. (0060546077). 256 pgs. When Evan, his mother, and young sister move into a rickety old house that needs a lot of care, Evan finds another inhabitant. Cora, the ghost of a girl who lived in the house over 100 years ago, still lives there. She writes poetry and admires Evan from afar. Once she begins to appear in his dreams he begins to question his relationship with her. A coming-of-age tale with love and lust. BBYA (nominated 2007)

❑ Johnson, Harriet McBryde. *Accidents of Nature.* (2006) Holt. (0805076344). 240 pgs. Jean has spent all of her 17 years with her cerebral palsy and has never met another person like her until she arrives at Camp Courage. Her friendship with Sara, a wheelchair bound camper, changes her outlook on life. Together they ask questions about race, feminism, identity, and sexuality, and what is normal? PW; SLJ; BBYA (nominated 2007)

❑ Johnson, Marilyn. *The Dead Beat: Lost Souls, Lucky Stiffs and the Perverse Pleasures of Obituaries.* (2006) HarperCollins. (0060758759). 256 pgs. Marilyn Johnson has written obituaries of Princess Di and Johnny Cash and spends numerous hours studying the craft. There is humor and claims that we are in the "golden age" of the obituary. Non-fiction; BBYA (nominated 2007)

❑ Johnson, Maureen. *13 Little Blue Envelopes.* (2005) HarperCollins, 2005. (0060541415). 336 pgs. After Aunt Peg dies of cancer, her niece gets the first of 13 blue envelopes. And with that envelope Ginny begins a journey through Europe—a journey that will give her own life a new perspective. BBYA (2006); BCCB; PW

❑ Jones, Patrick. *Nailed.* (2006) Walker. (0802780776). 224 pgs. Even his father bullies him. The jocks at school are ruthless. But now that Bret, 16, is performing with a band and acting, he hopes that his father and the jocks will stop the bullying. BBYA (nominated 2007)

❑ Jurmain, Suzanne. *The Forbidden Schoolhouse: The True and Dramatic Story of Prudence Crandall and Her Students.* (2005) Houghton. Illustrated. (0618473025). Crandall faced opposition of many of the townspeople in Canterbury, Connecticut when she, a white woman, opened a school for African-American girls (1833). Non-fiction; BBYA (2006); BCCB

❑ Kadohata, Cynthia. *Weedflower.* (2006) Simon & Schuster/Atheneum (0689865740). 272 pgs. After Pearl Harbor, twelve-year-old Sumiko, and her family are forced to leave their California flower farm and are interred in a camp on a Mohave reservation in Arizona. BBYA (nominated 2007); SLJ

Book Note

Include *Weedflower* in a collaborative reading list focusing on World War II. See "Picture Books and Historical Novels for World War II" (Online) www.mcelmeel.com/curriculum/picturebooks_WWII.html for other citations.

❑ Kibuishi, Kazu. *Daisy Kutter: The Last Train.* (2005) Viper Comics. (0975419323). 192 pgs. Daisy Kutter is a reformed bandit and a small-town model citizen where her ex-partner in crime and love is now the sheriff. She was a model citizen until she loses her general store in a poker game. And then the lure of the ultimate heist unfolds. Graphic Novel; BBYA (2006)

❑ Kidd, Ronald. *Monkey Town: The Summer of the Scopes Trial*. (2006) Simon & Schuster. (1416905723). 272 pgs. Against a backdrop of the famous Scopes "Monkey Trial" pitting attorneys Clarence Darrow and William Jennings Bryan are against one another and unending media attention, 15-year-old Frances begins to examine her own beliefs and relationships with her family and community. BBYA (nominated 2007); BCCB, Kirkus; SLJ

❑ Krovatin, Christopher. *Heavy Metal and You*. (2005) Scholastic/Push. (043973648X). 192 pgs. Laced with music references (including Metalhead album release dates and so forth), slang, and raw language, this tale is the classic bad boy meets good girl and finds that to keep the girl he must change—does he? Or can he? BBYA (2006); Booklist

❑ Kuhlman, Evan. *Wolf Boy: A Novel*. (2006) Random House/Shaye Areheart. (0307336964). 320 pgs. An inventive book that recounts Stephen's efforts to rescue his dysfunctional family after his older brother dies. Stephen channels his efforts into creating the superhero Wolfboy. His rather unique girlfriend Nicole collaborates with him and creates the illustrations as Stephen attempts to grapple with saving the world. A unique perspective and execution of a struggle to save his life. BBYA (nominated 2007)

❑ Lake, Sanoe. *Surfer Girl: A Guide to the Surfing Life*. (2005) Little, Brown. (0316110159). 144 pgs. Everything you ever wanted to know about surfing and more. Hazards in the sea to fashions to wear while on the surf board. Learn the language of surfers and how to select equipment and hints for riding the waves. VOYA Non-fiction

❑ Lansens, Lori. *The Girls: A Novel*. (2006) Little, Brown. (0316069035). 352 pgs. 29-year-old conjoined twins Ruby and Rose each tell their version of their autobiography. Conjoined at the side of their head, the girls were abandoned by their unwed teen mother who gave birth to them in a small town outside of Toronto. Adopted by the nurse who assisted in their birth, the two have been loved and raised in the Ontario countryside. But the love of their adoptive parents cannot protect them from Frankie Foyle who takes their virginity, the humiliation they sometimes experience, or the medical prognosis for a shorter life than normal. That prognosis spurs Rose to begin her story and to prod the reluctant Ruby to do the same. Alternating voices. BBYA (nominated 2007); Booklist

❑ Larbalestier, Justine. *Magic or Madness*. (2005) Penguin/Razorbill. (1595140220). 288 pgs. For years Reason and her mother have avoided her grandmother. But Reason's mother is mentally ill, and Reason, now fifteen, must live with her grandmother. Reason finds that her grandmother really is a witch and that her own body holds the same genes. But to use the witch's magic will bring a high price. BBYA (2006); Booklist; BCCB; SLJ

❑ Larochelle, David. *Absolutely Positively Not*. (2005) Scholastic/Arthur A. Levine. (0439591090). 224 pgs. Coming out as a teenager is difficult, and Steven is not really sure he is gay, but his new health teacher is very handsome. Humorous. Sid Fleischman Humor Award; BBYA (2006); BCCB; Booklist

❑ Lester, Julius. *Day of Tears: A Novel in Dialogue*. (2005) Hyperion/Jump at the Sun. (0786804904). 92 pgs. Emma and Joe struggle with the idea of escape after they become chattel and are sold at the largest slave auction in American history. BBYA (2006); SLJ; Booklist

Lester, Julius. ***This Strange New Feeling: Three Love Stories from Black History***. (2007) Dial. (978080373172). 193 pgs. On the 25th anniversary of publication, Dial is reissuing this volume of three stories that speak of personal freedom. The first story is that of Ras and Sally who find the strange new feeling after successfully fleeing after Ras's involvement in leading slaves to freedom is uncovered. The second story tells of a freed slave who works as a ferrier but is killed by the kick of a horse, and his enslaved wife is sold back into slavery to pay his debts. The third story is that of Ellen and William Craft and how Ellen posed as a white man traveling with her male slave (William) and traveled north to freedom on the train.

Book Note: Ellen and William Craft
Pair this story with ***5,000 Miles to Freedom: Ellen and William Craft's Flight From Slavery*** by Fradin, Judith Bloom and Dennis Brindell Fradin. (National Geographic, 2006)

Lester, Julius. ***Time's Memory***. (2006) Farrar, Straus and Giroux. (0374371784). 240 pgs. Brought as a seed on a slave ship, the life force emerges in the new land. Visualized in Ekundayo, he is transported to Virginia in the body of the young slave, Nathaniel. A love interest develops between Nathaniel and Ellen, the master's daughter, who has taught him to read and write. He struggles to discover how he can bring peace to the gray fog (the stories and tribulations of dead slaves) hovering over the slave quarters. When he is able to envision the past and foresee a course for future generations, he is brought the promise of peace, acceptance, and happiness. BBYA (nominated 2007); BCCB; PW

Author Note
More about Julius Lester online at http://members.authorsguild.net/juliuslester/

Levithan, David. ***Are We There Yet?*** (2005) Knopf. (037582846X). 224 pgs. Two brothers, Elijah and Danny, are as different as night and day. But their parents, who hope they will rekindle their positive relationship, send them on an Italian trip. Elijah meets Julia, and as that attraction blossoms Julia meets Danny. BBYA (2006)

Levithan, David. ***Marly's Ghost***. (2006) Penguin Goup USA/Dial. (0803730632). 176 pgs. The Valentine Day's celebration in his small town is painful as Ben recalls the death of his girlfriend, Marly, from cancer. Four spirits (including that of Marly) take Ben back into the past to remember his love of Marly, to the present to examine his present sorrow, and into the future where he sees himself committing suicide—that is unless he can become strong enough to stop himself. Written by the author of *Boy Meets Boy* (2003), this title also involves gay relationships. BBYA (nominated 2007)

Lipsyte, Robert. ***Heroes of Baseball: The Men Who Made it America's Favorite Game***. (2006) Simon & Schuster/Atheneum. (0689867417). 96 pgs. The history of baseball and the major-league heroes that made the game, including but not limited to household names: "Big Al" Spalding, Ty Cobb, Mark McGuire, Sammy Sosa, Curt Flood, who challenged the reserve clause, and Ichiro Suzuki, a player with one of the most thrilling "rookie" years in Seattle. Incidental information covers baseball cards, nicknames, mascots and other interesting pieces of baseball information. Non-fiction; BBYA (nominated 2007)

❑ Lisle, Janet Taylor. ***Black Duck***. (2006) Penguin Group USA/Philomel/Sleuth. (0399239634). 240 pgs. David is determined to be published in his local newspaper. While writing a story about the legendary and mysterious deaths surrounding the 1929 rum-running ship, he comes to the door of aging Ruben Hart. Mob action, prohibition, and unsolved mysteries populate Hart's tale of his past and involvement with the mystery. Both Ruben and David want to bring the truth to light. Staying honest is hard to do. BBYA (nominated 2007); SLJ

❑ Lubar, David. ***Sleeping Freshmen Never Lie: A Novel.*** (2005) Dutton. (0525473114). 160 pgs. He is the least athletic sports reporter that his high school newspaper has ever had. He runs for student council, tries out for plays, but is chided by the seniors. Meanwhile, his mother is pregnant and, to help him survive, he writes his unborn sibling some sage advice for surviving the freshman year. Humorous diary entries. BCCB Blue Ribbon Fiction Book. BBYA (2006); BCCB; SLJ

❑ Lynch, Chris. ***Inexcusable***. (2005) Simon & Schuster/Atheneum. (0689847890). 176 pgs. Keir Sarafina knows how to rationalize his bad behavior: destroy a town statue is just a prank, getting drunk is just silly, and even using drugs is just recreational. But date raping the girl you say you love—inexcusable. Gigi sees the situation in the same way Sam does. Throughout this story Keir tries to convince readers that he really is a good guy. BBYA2006-Top10 BBYA (2006); Kirkus; PW; SLJ; SLJ Best Books

❑ Lynch, Jim. ***The Highest Tide: A Novel.*** (2005) Bloomsbury. (1-58234-605-4). 272 pgs. Set in Puget Sound, Miles O'Malley, discovers life at high tide and a remarkable summer. BBYA (2006); PW

❑ Mackall, Dandi Daley. ***Eva Underground: A Novel.*** (2006) Harcourt, 2006. (0152054626). 256 pgs. Eva's mother died of cancer in 1978, the year her father decided to escape their Chicago home and work with the Polish underground education movement. Of course, Eva must accompany him and desperately misses her friends and social life. She botches an attempt to return home but finds a friendship with the underground leader Tomek. A candid look inside a Communist country and the despair of the Polish people. She is there to witness hope develop as Lech Walesa and the Solidarity Movement rise to power, and the world elects the first Polish pope. BBYA (nominated 2007); Kirkus

❑ Marino, Peter. ***Dough Boy***. (2005) Holiday House. (0823418731). 221 pgs. As long as his mother's boyfriend, Frank, was overweight and his father's girlfriend bordered on the fat side, Tristan's own existence as a fat boy did not cause him concern. He was even shielded from bullying at school by his best friend Marco's popularity. Tristan spent alternating weeks with his mother and college-professor father. It was a situation that worked until Frank's calorie conscious bully daughter moved in. Her mouth was ruthless as she attacked Tristan with esteem-cutting remarks. When her disdain begins to elicit tormenting comments from other students at school, he realizes that he must remove himself from the situation. Blended families, bullying, and an effort to regain and build self-esteem are all topics that will engage many readers. BBYA (nominated 2007); BCCB; PW

❑ Marsalis, Wynton. ***Jazz A-B-Z: An A to Z Collection of Jazz Portraits***. (2005) Illustrated by Paul Rogers. Candlewick. (0763621358). 76 pgs. Twenty-six Jazz greats are included in alliterative poetry. Rogers' large illustrations illuminate the poems.

> **Book Notes: Fat Characters in Literature**
>
> Add ***Dough Boy*** to a collaborative reading list that includes: *Fat Kid Rules the World* by K.L. Going (2003); *The Earth, My Butt, and Other Big Round Things* by Carolyn Mackler (2003), *One Fat Summer* by Robert Lipsyte (1982), *Staying Fat for Sarah Byrnes* by Chris Crutcher (2003 pb). For some insight into the "fat" characters used in YA books, read "Fat Characters in Recent Young Adult Fiction" from ***Kliatt*** (September 2003) by Rebecca Rabinowitz. Linked from http://www.mcelmeel.com/curriculum/litwww.html

❑ McGhee, Alison. **All Rivers Flow to the Sea**. (2005) Candlewick. (0763625914). 176 pgs. Ivy (18) and Rose (17) have been as close as anyone could be—secrets, high school, boyfriends—and then comes that fateful night. Rose is left to tell the story, "Ivy and I had an accident..." and Ivy is left on life support. Readers will grieve with Ivy and get an inner look at family dynamics in the face of tragedy. BBYA (2006); BCCB; PW

❑ McKillip, Patricia A. **Solstice Wood**. (2006) Penguin Group USA/Ace. (044101366X). 288 pgs. Sylvia managed to leave the pull of the faery world behind when she left her grandparents' home seven years ago. But the barrier between the worlds has weakened while she has been gone, and when she returns for her grandfather's funeral the treacherous pull of the old house and the shadowy forest brings her to the "bridge across the boundary." Can she resist or can she bring a measure of trust and a new peace between faery and human worlds? BBYA (nominated 2007)

❑ Menzel, Peter and Faith D'Aluisio. **Hungry Planet: What the World Eats**. (2005) Ten Speed Press. (1580086810). 288 pgs. Thirty families in 24 countries purchase a week's worth of food—food that costs a mother and five children in Chad $1.44 a week to a German family of four spending $494.19. Questions surrounding the lists of food, quantities, and health are included. Very provocative. Non-fiction; BBYA (nominated 2007)

❑ Meyer, Stephanie. **Twilight: A Novel**. (2005) Little, Brown/Megan Tingley. (0316160172). 512 pgs. Star-crossed lovers—Bella meets Edward. His vampire urges are difficult to hold back; for Bella the consequences might be deadly. And then a roving band of vampires fixate on her. BBYA2006-Top10 BBYA (2006); PW; SLJ

❑ Miller, Kirsten. **Kiki Strike: Inside the Shadow City**. (2006) Bloomsbury. (1582349606). 250 pgs. The first in a series about a group of girls who protect New York City's secret underground world, *The Shadow City*. Ananka Fishbein is the mastermind who leads the Irregulars, a group of five girls who join her fight. Ananka has her own set of rules. The Irregulars' obsession with boys, looks, and the glorious life have moved into the real world and built an existence filled with adventure and excitement. (Annotation adapted from *Young Adult Literature and Multimedia: A Quick Guide, 2nd edition*. Hi-Willow, 2006.)

Author Note

Kristen Miller says her characters have "strength [that] comes from what's inside their heads, not what's inside their bras." (quoted from: TeenRead.com. "Interview with Kristen Miller. Online. URL: www.teenreads.com/authors/au-miller-kirsten.asp#view060601 BBYA (nominated 2007)

❏ Miller, Mary Beth. **On the Head of a Pin**. (2006) Penguin Group USA/Dutton. (0525477365). 256 pgs. Helen and her boyfriend are at a party at Andy's father's isolated cabin. Michael passes out, and Helen is upstairs when Andy points a gun and accidentally kills Helen as she descends the stairs. Andy's pal Josh wants to call 911 but in the end Josh and Victor (another boy at the party) help Andy bury the body on a neighbor's property. Anguish and guilt besiege the boys but not enough to keep them from involving Michael in the aftermath of their "accident." Teens, guns, and consequences. Pair with Walter Dean Myers's *Monster* (1999) or *Shooter* (2004); and Nancy Garden's *Endgame* (2006). BBYA (nominated 2007); Booklist; BCCB

❏ Mitchell, David. **Black Swan Green**. (2006) Random House. (1400063795). 304 pgs. Unlike his earlier titles, this tale has but one narrator, one viewpoint, and is written as a first-person semiautobiographical coming-of-age story. 13-yeare-old Jason Taylor focuses on one year (1982) in Worcestershire's Black Swan Green. His family (smart older sister, sarcastic mother, and brisk father) populate the story along with bullies who taunt him. Jason's weakness is his stammer. Some days "N" words plague him, other days it might be "S" words. Once his classmates figure out what is going on, he is harassed mercilessly. But, in the end, Jason makes a discovery that will make readers who love adventure take notice. BBYA (nominated 2007); PW

❏ Moranville, Sharelle Byars. **A Higher Geometry**. (2006) Henry Holt. (0805074708). 224 pgs. Set in the Midwest during the Cold War (post World War II), Anna is determined to pursue her mathematical career. Set apart from her female classmates most of her classes are dominated by males— males who consider her an oddity but not a serious contender in the world of mathematics. Then Anna finds Mike, as artistically talented as she is in the mathematical field. Their frank discussions about sex, faith, and life's goals and successes contribute to her determination to succeed in the world of numbers. BBYA (nominated 2007)

❏ Murdock, Catherine Gilbert. **Dairy Queen**. (2006) Houghton Mifflin. (0618683070). 278 pgs. Saddled with the major portion of the work on her family's Wisconsin dairy farm after her father's injury, D.J. is overwhelmed with all the duties necessary to keep the business running. In addition, the summer is focused on training Brian, an opposing high school quarterback. But D.J. is not a girly-girl, she is just a regular girl interested in sports and by the time fall and school comes around once again she decides to join her own high school football team. Funny, filled with sports, and engaging characters. BBYA (nominated 2007); Kirkus

Author Note

For more information about Moranville visit her website at http://www.sharellebyarsmoranville.com/ and learn about her first novel **Over the River** (Henry Holt, 2002).

❑ Myers, Walter Dean. ***Autobiography of My Dead Brother***. (2005) Illustrated by Christopher Myers. HarperCollins/Amistad. (006058291X). 224 pgs. 15-year-old Jesse is a talented artist and it is his art that helps him see his best friend Rise's drift into "fronting cool." A poignant look at how to survive hopelessness and the violence rooted in his neighborhood. BBYA (2006); BCCB; Kirkus; SLJ

❑ Myers, Walter Dean. ***Street Love***. (2006) Armistad. (0060280808). 144 pgs. When their mother is sentenced to 25 years in prison, Junice and her younger sister know that foster care is not far way. Their grandmother's home is not a solution and chances are the two girls will be separated. Junice is not sure about how to react to the arrival of Damien, a student-athlete. Junice's future is far from clear and Damien's future seems planned in every detail. What kind of a relationship can they have? And what of the future? A compelling verse novel.

❑ Na, An. ***Wait for Me***. (2006) Penguin Group USA/Putnam. (0399242759). 240 pgs. Mina's lies have convinced her mother, Uhmma, that she really can attend Harvard, but her senior year is unfolding and the lies will be discovered. Along the way brilliant Jonathan has helped her mold the lies by helping her forge her report cards. But he proves to be only self-centered as he rapes her and she turns to a Mexican immigrant that has come to work in her Korean family's dry cleaning business. Ysrael is a gifted musician and is on his way to San Francisco. Mina sees a way to escape her lies, find a place for herself, and once she ends up in California she finds her way. Unconventional punctuation. BBYA (nominated 2007); Booklist

❑ Nelson, Marilyn. ***A Wreath for Emmett Till***. (2005) Illustrated by Philippe Lardy. Houghton, 2005. (0618397523). 48 pgs. A heroic crown of sonnets describe the death of 14-year-old Emmett Till and places Till's death in historic context. Nonfiction BBYA (2006); Booklist; Kirkus; PW; SLJ

❑ Nelson, Marilyn. ***Fortune's Bones: The Manumission Requiem***. (2004) Front Street. Illustrated. (1932425128). 32 pgs. The bones of Fortune, a slave, are immortalized by the poetic words of Nelson as she describes his body's dissection and rendering of his skeleton by his master. His skeleton is then put on display in a museum. Nonfiction BBYA (2006); SLJ

Author Note

Marilyn Nelson was named poet laureate for the state of Connecticut in 2001. She is a professor emeritus at the University of Connecticut and has become a valued and respected poet. She opens up her home as a poets' retreat three times a year – Soul Mountain Retreat. Find out more at http://www.soulmountainretreat.com

❑ Nolan, Han. ***A Summer of Kings***. (2006) Harcourt. (0152051082). 352 pgs. It is the summer of 1963. This is the summer Ester will rebel. It is also the summer King-Roy, the 18-year-old son of her mother's childhood friend, comes up from Alabama to live with her family. He is escaping accusations that he murdered a white man. King-Roy becomes a defender of Malcolm X and the Nation of Islam; Esther focuses on the principles of James Baldwin, Dr. Martin Luther King, and Mahatma Gandi. Humor, vibrant exchanges of philosophies, and subtle prejudice fueled in part by a touch of romance. BBYA (nominated 2007); Kirkus; SLJ

❑ O'Donnell, Joe. *Japan 1945: A U.S. Marine's Photographs from Ground Zero.* (2005) Vanderbilt. Illustrated. (0826514677). 87 pgs. Through the eyes of an unflinching camera, readers are given a unique visual perspective on the devastation of Ground Zero in Japan as seen shortly after the bombing of Hiroshima and Nagasaki. Non-fiction; BBYA (2006)

❑ Oppel, Kenneth. *Skybreaker.* (2005) HarperCollins/Eos. (0060532270). 384 pgs. A fantasy space novel. Matt Cruise and his fellow Airship Academy training students sight a long-lost treasure-laden spaceship. Once the ship's sighting is known, a race to reach the ship first and take the treasure is undertaken. Matt ends up aboard a vessel with his old friend Kate—a mysterious young woman and a rogue adventurer—seeking the treasure before the space pirates reach the treasure ship. BBYA (2006)

❑ Oppenheim, Joanne. *Dear Miss Breed: True Stories of the Japanese American Incarceration During World War II and a Librarian Who Made a Difference.* (2006) Scholastic Nonfiction. (0439569923). 288 pgs. A public librarian, Miss Breed, made sure that the Japanese-American children who were interred in concentration camps were sent books during their incarceration during World War II. Non-fiction; BBYA (nominated 2007); Booklist

---

Connections—Librarians: Books to Children
Read more books about librarians who make a difference. (Online) www.mcelmeel.com/curriculum/librarians.html

---

❑ Park, Linda Sue. *Project Mulberry.* (2005) Clarion. (0618477861). 240 pgs. Julia Song and her friend Patrick need a project for state fair. Will raising silk worms be "American" enough? A funny and witty presentation in which the author also shares information about the writing process. SLJ

Author Note

Linda Sue Park won the 2002 Newbery Medal for her book *A Single Shard* (2001). (Online) http://www.lindasuepark.com

---

❑ Park, Linda Sue. *Archer's Quest.* (2006) Clarion. (0618596313). 176 pgs. When one of Korea's legendary great archers (from the first century B.C.) shows up Kevin's bedroom, the fun has just begun. Kevin, a sixth grader in Dorchester, NY, has to help Chu-mong return to his home (and century) before the Year of the Tiger ends on the following day—and all of history is changed. Interspersed throughout the book is much Korean history, and bits and pieces of the culture that Kevin learns to appreciate. Kevin also comes to realize that there is much to appreciate about his dad, a programmer at a local university, and one who loves math and precision.

❑ Partridge, Elizabeth. *John Lennon: All I Want Is the Truth.* (2005) Viking. (0670059544). 256 pgs. John Lennon in a revealing photo-biography. Strips away the myth of Lennon and presents the man who sought truth through music. A birth to death biography that includes much information about his days with the Beatles. Non-fiction; BCCB Blue Ribbon nonfiction; BBYA (2006); Booklist

❏ Payment, Simone. *The Pony Express: A Primary Source History of the Race to Bring Mail to the American West*. (2005) Rosen. (1404201815) Primary source materials dealing with the basic information and time lines for the westward movement period of United States history, involving the brief 1-2 years that the pony express was in existence. Part of the Primary Sources in America History series. VOYA Non-fiction

❏ Pearson, Mary E. *A Room on Lorelei Street*. (2005) Holt. (0805076670). 272 pgs. Zoe must escape from her alcoholic mother, her overbearing grandmother, school, everything. The room on Lorelei Street provides a safe haven, but now Zoe must find a way to pay for the room. Zoe doesn't always make the "right" decisions but in the end she survives. The story is in the struggle to learn how. Golden Kite Award. BBYA (2006)

❏ Peck, Richard. *Here Lies the Librarian*. (2006) Penguin Group USA/Dial. (0803730802). 160 pgs. Peewee (Eleanor) McGrath, a 14-year-old tomboy, idolizes her older brother, Jake. The two are parentless but Jake manages by running a small garage. Set in rural Indiana, the story begins as a tornado rips through the countryside, disturbing the graveyard but not daring to upheave the stern former librarian's grave. The town's library has been closed since her death—but that just might change when Irene Ridpath shows up in a fancy car. BBYA (nominated 2007)

❏ Peck, Richard. *Past Perfect, Present Tense*. (2006) Viking. (014240537X). 192 pages. A reissue of Peck's collection of short stories, this edition includes eleven previously published short stories and two brand-new ones. Peck's first short story, "Shotgun Cheatham's Last Night Above Ground," inspired both *A Long Way from Chicago* and *A Year Down Yonder*, and "The Electric Summer," which was the inspiration for *Fair Weather*. Inside notes about his writing and tips for other writers.

❏ Peet, Mal. *Keeper*. (2005) Candlewick. (0763627496). 240 pgs. El Gato is at the top of his soccer game and everyone wants his story. His early life includes a remote South American village, the secret soccer field carved from the rain forest, and the mysterious figure he knows only as the Keeper who trained him. A fast-paced sports fantasy. 2004 Brandford Boase Award (UK), Nestle Children's Book Prize short list, BBYA (2006)

❏ Pemberton, Delia. *The Atlas of Ancient Egypt: With Artworks and Photographs from the British Museum*. (2005) Harry N. Abrams. (0810957965) 96 pgs. Very readable narrative showcasing holdings in the British Museum: maps, sidebars of information, glossary, and index. VOYA Non-fiction

❏ Perkins, Lynne Rae. *Criss Cross*. (2005) Greenwillow. illus. (0060092726). 352 pgs. A collection of connecting vignettes about Debbie and her friends. The title comes from a radio show, Criss Cross, which becomes a metaphor for these stories that show how one life intersects with another as they leave childhood behind. Funny, perceptive. Newbery Medal 2006 BBYA (2006); Booklist; BCCB; Horn Book; SLJ

❏ Peters, Julie Ann. *Between Mom and Jo*. (2006) Little Brown. (0316739065). 240 pgs. Nick has grown up in a household with two moms and everything has been fine until now. Mom and Jo are having problems and Nick is caught in the middle—in the middle of their break-up, his mom's new relationship, the battle of who he will live with, and his own emotions. SLJ

❑ Portman, Frank. *King Dork*. (2006) Random House/Delacorte. (0385732910). 352 pgs. 14-year-old Tom Henderson is on the popular girls' list of duds. Other humiliations come too. He takes refuge in his music and often composes songs. When he finds his father's copy of *The Catcher in the Rye* (and other books) he sets out to read each one and solve the clues left by his father; perhaps he can solve the mystery of his father's death. Popular culture, high school customs, literary criticism, and music all play a part in Tom's journey to self-realization. BBYA (nominated 2007); BCCB; Kirkus; SLJ

❑ Price, Charlie. *Dead Connection*. (2006) Roaring Brook. (1596431148). 240 pgs. Murray Kiefer is a loner and often spends solitary time in the town's cemetery. Pearl lives with her widowed father, the cemetery's caretaker. And then there is Nikki Parker—a teen who has disappeared. When Murray hears voices asking for help, he is set into motion, reluctantly befriending Pearl and start a quest to solve the murder mystery they have stumbled across. How long will it take them to figure out who is the "good" cop, who is the "bad" cop, and how bad is bad. Most violence takes place off-stage. A great mystery. BBYA (nominated 2007)

❑ Qualey, Marsha. *Just Like That*. (2005) Dial. (0803728409). 240 pgs. A chance encounter along Lake Calhoun and the death of two teens bring guilt and cause18-year-old Hanna to question her life and relationships—and her family and friends to wonder what has caused Hanna to retreat inside herself. BBYA (2006)

❑ Reinhardt, Dana. *A Brief Chapter in My Impossible Life*. (2006) Random House/Wendy Lamb. (0385746989). 240 pgs. Simone is olive skinned, her family fair skinned. She's always known she was adopted and really has not cared to meet her birth mother. But now at age 16, her birth mother, a 33 year-old self-exiled Hasidic Jewish woman, has ovarian cancer and she wants to meet Simone. Reluctantly Simone agrees to meet Rivka. Knowing one another gives each of them something to hold to but it also turns Simone's year upside down. Simone must learn how to balance her place in two families, a love life, deal with academic responsibilities, learning how to stand up for herself, and keeping her place in her high school culture. Big issues to contend with while coming-of-age. BBYA (nominated 2007); BCCB; PW; SLJ

❑ Richardson, Nigel. *The Wrong Hands*. (2006) Random House/Alfred A. Knopf. (0375834591). 272 pgs. 14-year-old Graham Sinclair's secret was not intended to be revealed, but an e-mail changes all of that. Telling the secret only brings him trouble. His disfigured (and huge) hands make him the butt of bullying but it is ability to fly that he must keep secret. When a ruthless journalist gets a hold of the information, Graham is in for a big fall. Part allegory, part fantasy, and extremely compelling. BBYA (nominated 2007)

❑ Riordan, Rick. *The Lightning Thief: Percy Jackson and the Olympians.* (2005) Hyperion. (0786856297). 384 pgs. Percy is just another ADHD kid in boarding school for troubled teenagers, until he finds out who he really is—the Son of Poseidon and a mortal woman. Now in mortal danger, he strikes out to find his own place in the 21st century. BBYA (2006); SLJ

❑ Rosoff, Meg. ***Just in Case***. (2006) Random House/Wendy Lamb. (0385746784). 256 pgs. When David saves his baby brother by rescuing him from the window's ledge, he knows fate has intervened. Convinced that fate has more in store for him, he sets out to change his total identity, starting with a new name and a new wardrobe. Soon it is clear that fate will actually speak to him. A love interest, friendships, and an examination of faith, time, free will, and the boundaries of love and sex make this a provocative read. BBYA (nominated 2007)

❑ Rowling, J. K. ***Harry Potter and the Half-Blood Prince***. (2005) Illustrated by Mary GrandPré. Scholastic/Arthur A. Levine. (0439784549). 652 pgs. Book 6 takes Harry into even darker adventures and he moves into being contrary, less trusting, and into seeking revenge. BBYA (2006); BCCB; Booklist; PW

❑ Sachar, Louis. ***Small Steps***. (2006) Delacorte. (0385733143). 272 pgs. A continuation of sorts of the story told in ***Holes*** (1998). Armpit, a former resident of Tent D at Camp Green Lake is the focus of this story. He's still digging holes but now for a landscaper in Austin, Texas. Others do not expect him to succeed, but he has faith and knows that if he just takes one small step at a time he will move forward. X-ray is still his friend and together they manage to save a young girl. Humor and social commentary abound in this tale from a master storyteller. Booklist

---

📖 Author Note

Louis Sachar's ***Holes*** was awarded the 1999 Newbery Medal. More about Sachar's other books and about the author at (online): http://www.louissachar.com/

❑ Salisbury, Graham. ***Eyes of the Emperor***. (2005) Random/Wendy Lamb. (0385729715). 240 pgs. Eddy Okubo wants to serve his country and lies about his age to join the U.S. Army in 1941. Despite facing extreme racism, Eddy persists as he joins young Japanese American men training experimental K-9 units to hunt Japanese during World War II. Companion novel to *Under the Blood-Red Sun* (1995). BBYA (2006)

❑ Schlosser, Eric and Charles Wilson. ***Chew On This: Everything You Don't Want to Know About Fast Food***. (2006) Houghton Mifflin. (0618710310). 270 pgs. All you ever wanted to know, or not know, about fast food—interviews, statistics, and little known information. Non-fiction; BBYA (nominated 2007); Booklist

❑ Schmemann, Serge. ***New York Times: When the Wall Came Down: The Berlin Wall and the Fall of Communism***. (2006) Larousse/Kingfisher. (07534359949). 128 pgs. As a veteran journalist in Germany at the time the wall fell, Schmemann tells the immediate story of the fall of the wall from his experience and then recounts the history of the Berlin Wall—how it came to be and the events that lead to it's dismantling. The complete story is gripping and one of the major events in European history. Non-fiction; PW

❑ Shull, Megan. ***Amazing Grace***. (2005) Hyperion. (0786856904). 256 pgs. Followed by paparazzi, world tennis star Grace "Ace" Kincaid wants out. She calls her mother from the US Open and insists she is done. In short order her Aunt Ava, a retired FBI agent, spirits her away to a cabin in Medicine Hat, Alaska. Her first venture into town has her colliding with a moose and meeting a friendly local boy, Teague. Set in new surroundings, Grace finds her own way and a new real self. BBYA (nominated 2007)

❏ Shulman, Polly. *Enthusiasm.* (2006) Penguin Group USA/Putnam (0399243895). 212 pgs. Julie and Ashleigh are Jane Austen fans and best friends. Each is looking for a first love. Julie has spotted her Mr. Darcy at the mall. Convinced that she will find him if she crashes the local boys' prep school, Julia convinces Ashleigh to go with her. They find him, but when Ashleigh is also attracted to the same boy, frustrating and confusing times follow. BBYA (nominated 2007); Booklist; BCCB

❏ Sizer, Paul. *Moped Army*. (2006) Café Digital Comics/Fiery Studios. (0976856549). 144 pgs. Simmering socio-political ideas begin to surface when a clash between two rival groups takes Simone from the "upper" society to experiencing life in the Lower City with the Moped Army. Story takes place in the latter part of the 23rd century. BBYA (nominated 2007)

❏ Skelton, Matthew. *Endymion Spring*. (2006) Random House/Delacorte. (0385733801). 400 pgs. Set at Oxford University, Blake finds himself a target of members of the antiquarian book society who want an important writing fragment for themselves. The fragment is revealed to have connections to the original 15th century printing press. A scholarly background that will appeal mostly to bibliophiles. BBYA (nominated 2007)

❏ Sloan, Christopher. *How Dinosaurs Took Flight: Fossils, Science, What We Think We Know, and Mysteries Yet Unsolved.* (2005) National Geography. (079227298) Documents the research concerned with the connections between dinosaurs and birds. Photographs illuminate the hypotheses and evidence presented to support the contention that birds evolved beyond the dinosaurs. VOYA Non-fiction

❏ Smith, Greg Leitich. *Tofu and T.Rex.* (2005) Little Brown. (0316777226). 176 pgs. After being kicked out of a Texas school, militant vegan Frederika Murchison-Kowalski is back at the Peshtigo School. She must live with her cousin Hans-Peter and their Opa. Constantly at odds with one another, Hans-Peter needs Freddie or he may not get into Peshtigo School. The two cousins are eighth graders but act more like sixth graders. A good solid school and family tale. Companion to *Ninjas, Piranhas, and Galileo* (2004)

❏ Smith, Kirsten. *The Geography of Girlhood*. (2006) Little, Brown. (0316160210). 192 pgs. Penny's mother abandoned her when she was just six. Now in high school Penny still longs for her mother but also has to deal with adolescence: a depressed friend, her first boyfriend's accidental death, an older and wild sister, a new step-mother. It seems like everything in her life is a mistake, including her decision to run away with her sister's ex-boyfriend. Coming home, she finds that there is more to life than what she has seen so far. A verse novel. BBYA (nominated 2007)

❏ Sonneborn, Liz. *The Mexican-American War: A Primary Source History of the Expansion of the Western Lands of the United States.* (2005) Rosen. (1404201807) Primary source materials dealing with the basic information and time lines for the westward movement period of United States history. Part of the Primary Sources in America History series. VOYA Non-fiction

❑ Spiegler, Louise. *The Amethyst Road*. (2005) Houghton Mifflin/Clarion. (0618485724). 336 pgs. Born of an Anglo father and a Gypsy mother, Serena and her sister, Willow, are outcasts in both cultures in their neighborhood in the city of Oestia. The Anglo culture rejects them because of their Yulang blood and the Yulang culture rejects them because Serena's niece, Zara, was born out of wedlock. But when Zara is taken by Child Protective Services, Serena realizes that if her family is to be reunited it will be up to her—and she must seek help wherever she can find it. BBYA (nominated 2007)

❑ Spillebeen, Geert. *Kipling's Choice*. (2005) Translated by Terese Edelstein. Houghton. (0618431241). 160 pgs. Lt. John Kipling's famous father, Rudyard Kipling, has used his influence to get the authorities to allow John, despite poor eyesight, to join the British Army in World War I. And now he lies dying in France. A gripping story contrasting the war and the home front. BCCB Blue Ribbon Fiction Books; BBYA (2006); SLJ

❑ Staples, Suzanne Fisher. *Under the Persimmon Tree*. (2005) Farrar/ Frances Foster. (0374380252). 288 pgs. Set in Afghanistan, a young girl loses her mother and brother in an air raid. Her father and brother are conscripted into the army. But Najmah seeks refuge in Pakistan with an American-Muslim teacher (Elaine/Nusrat). BBYA (2006); Booklist; BCCB; PW

❑ Stassen, Jean-Philippe. *Deogratias, a Tale of Rwanda.* (2006) Roaring Brook/First Second. (1596431032). 96 pgs. Deogratias is a teenaged Hutu; his friends Benina and Apollinaria are Tutsi. But Deogratias and his love Benina cannot be together. The brutality and atrocities of the Rwandan genocide are not fully shared, but scenes of rape, harsh language, and some sexual content render this graphically designed account of Rwanda's history will be more suitable for a mature audience. A gripping graphic novel. BBYA (nominated 2007); PW

❑ Stein, Tammar. *Light Years: A Novel.* (2005) Knopf. (0375830235). 272 pgs. Virginia is to be a refuge for her grief and pain, but Maya Laor finds she cannot escape from the guilt she feels for the tragic suicide bombing that killed her boyfriend. Her past life in Israel and her life as an Astronomy student are light years apart. BBYA (2006)

❑ Stone, Tanya Lee. *A Bad Boy Can be Good for a Girl.* (2006) Random House/Wendy Lamb. (0385747020). 240 pgs. One sexy high school senior manages to seduce and then drop Josie, a freshman who values her girlfriends over boys; Nicolette who views her own sexuality as a point of power; and finally Aviva, a pretty, smart, and artsy senior. When he summarily dumps each of them, they begin to realize what love and sex is all about. A few blank pages at the end of the book holds handwritten notes that reveal each of their thoughts. Sex scenes (although not graphic) may make this more appropriate for mature readers—but given a chance it will be passed from teenage girl to teenage girl. Free verse. Use in connection with Judy Blume's *Forever.* BBYA (nominated 2007); SLJ

❑ Stroud, Jonathan. *Ptolemy's Gate*. (2005) Hyperion/Miramax. (0786818611). 512 pgs. The final book in the Bartimaeus Trilogy. Nathanial, an apprentice magician, calls upon Bartimaeus, a 5000 year old djinni. Nathanial is strong in face of the war against the most dangerous demons encountered to date. Kitty is a strong and intelligent hero, and all principals are part of an exciting conclusion to this triology. BBYA (nominated 2007)

❑ Sturtevant, Katherine. *A True and Faithful Narrative*. (2006) Farrar Straus Giroux. (0374378096). 256 pgs. Famous authors and poets visit Meg Moore's father's bookstore frequently and 16-year-old Meg spends hours in conversation with some of the most learned figures in London. She no longer plans to inherit her father's bookstore since he has remarried and now has a son, but she still clings to her hopes of overcoming the 17th century disapproval of female authors. Her best friend, Anne, is in an unhappy marriage and Anne's brother (who seems to have been in love with Meg) has set sail for Italy. On his return trip, the ship is seized by pirates and Edward is sold as a slave in Algiers. It is at this point that Meg realizes that she must use the power of her pen. A gripping novel in which Meg finds solutions within the limitations 17th century society has placed on females. Sequel to *At the Sign of the Star* (2000). Booklist; SLJ

❑ Sullivan, George. *Bernice Abbott, Photographer: Independent Vision.* (2006) Clarion. (0618440267). 160 pgs. A significant biography of a pioneer female photographer who changed photography by her innovative methods, her realism, and her drive to succeed. Particularly well-known for her photographs of New York City and Paris, later in life her work also illustrated many scientific writings. Some of her inventions are still used by photographers. (Non-fiction). Kirkus; Booklist

❑ Sullivan, George. *Built to Last: Building America's Amazing Bridges, Dams, Tunnels, and Skyscrapers.* (2005) Scholastic. (0439517370). 128 pgs. Diagrams, photos, charts, and sidebars present the information about seventeen of the most amazing bridges, dams, tunnels, and skyscrapers built in America. Details about design and construction. VOYA Non-fiction.

❑ Tanaka, Shelley. *Mummies: The Newest, Coolest and Creepiest from Around the World.* (2005) Harry N. Abrams. (0810957973). 48 pgs. Everything to know about mummies from all over the world. Historical and scientific information in a well-written narrative. Readers will be interested to find out that mummies are not just from Egypt. VOYA Non-fiction

❑ Tiffany, Grace. *Ariel.* (2005) HarperCollins/Laura Geringer. (0060753277). 240 pgs. Ariel, a mysterious figure from Shakespeare's Tempest, has her story of dreams and lies and madness. BBYA (2006); Booklist

❑ Tingle, Rebecca. *Far Traveler.* (2005) Putnam. (0399238905). 228 pgs. In this sequel to *The Edge on the Sword*, Aelfwyn finds herself vulnerable after the sudden death of her mother, Aethelflaed of Mercia. She must find a way to avoid a forced marriage to the king's ally, an older man. Fleeing, disguised as a male storyteller, Aelfwyn knows that the decisions she makes now will decide her future (and that of the Mercians). BBYA (2006)

❑ Tullson, Diane. *Red Sea.* (2005) Orca. (1551433311). 169 pgs. Libby, a 14-year-old, defies her step-father and mother at every turn. Their family is on a sailing voyage but when Libby is purposely late they miss setting sail with their flotilla— but decide to sail alone, intending to catch up. What they encounter are modern-day pirates, murder, serious injury—all leaving Libby terrified and responsible for the sailboat and getting her mother to help before she dies. BBYA (2006)

❑ Turner, Ann Warren. *Hard Hit.*. (2006) Scholastic. (0439296803). 1128 pgs. Matt's life seems enviable. He is a high-school basketball star, has a popular girlfriend, and a loyal best friend. Then the news comes—his father has pancreatic cancer and despite a brief remission he needs much care. Matt's life seems to stand still while his friends move on. When all is said and done, Matt still must deal with his immense grief and struggle to get his life back on track. Many resources appended. Kirkus

❑ Turner, Megan Whalen. *The King of Attolia.* (2006) HarperCollins/Greenwillow. (006083577X). 400 pgs. After marrying the Queen, Eugenides (King Gen), the former thief and liar, must convince the rest of the court that he is deserving of the title. Since it is the Queen who ordered Eugenides's hand cut off, the Attolian's find it difficult to believe that the two are truly in love—most feel she is using him. Most of the court feels that King Gen is spineless and mock him, but when one court guard goes too far and knocks him down, an infraction that is punishable by beheading, they find out that Eugenides is a shrewd king. Sequel to *The Queen of Attolia* (2000) and *The Thief* (1996). BBYA (nominated 2007); SLJ

❑ Vaughan, Brian K. *Runaways: Volume 1—Pride and Joy.* (2005) Illustrated by Adrian Alphona. Marvel. (0785118764). 448 pgs. The first in a series of exploits by six teenagers (a goth girl, the brain, the jock, the dreamboat, and the shy one) who discover that their parents don't just seem evil but actually are evil super-villains. Once they decide to turn their parents they must fight for their own survival and put an end to the evil that surrounds their family. First in a series of graphic novels. BBYA2006-Top10 BBYA (2006)

❑ Vaught, Susan. *Stormwitch*. (2005) Bloomsbury. (1582349525). 200 pgs. After her parents die, Ruba, leaves her native Haiti to move to Mississippi to be with her grandmother. But it is her recently deceased Haitian grandmother who has taught the 16-year-old to use chants, spells, and herbal potions to control her environment. Civil Rights, Hurricane Camille, and a white boy with a gun are all obstacles she meets with stubborn determination. A clash of cultures, beliefs, and pride. BBYA (2006)

❑ Vizzini, Ned. *It's Kind of a Funny Story*. (2006) Hyperion/Miramax. (0786851961). Depression plagues 15-year-old Craig as he pressures himself to maintain his image at the prestigious Manhattan high school. When he decides he is better and stops taking his medication, he slides even further and ends up in an adult psych ward. It is here that he gets the help he needs. The five-day stay is packed with episodes that might occur but not during such a compacted stay. BBYA (nominated 2007); Booklist

> **Connections—Dealing with Depression**
> For a look at depression (but not such a funny story) read: *Conquering the Beast Within: How I Fought Depression and Won... and How You Can, Too* by Cait Irwin (1999). This is Cait's own story of the depression she battled from the age of fourteen and into her adult life.

❑ Volponi, Paul. *Black and White.* (2005) Viking. (0-670-06006-2). 192 pgs. Best friends Marcus ("Black") and Eddie ("White") have gotten past the racial "crap." Both have been offered basketball scholarships from New York City colleges. But they need spending money and armed robberies seem to be the answer until on their third try the robbery goes terribly wrong and everything changes. Alternating voices. BBYA (2006); Booklist

❑ Volponi, Paul. *Rooftop.* (2006) Penguin Group USA/Viking. (0670060690). 208 pgs. Clay (17) has been estranged from his cousin Addison (18) but now both are going through a drug abuse program in New York City. Finally reconciling (for good or bad) Clay goes to the rooftop just in time to see a white officer shoot Addison. Was Addison going clean? Was the shooting a horrible mistake? What will this do to Clay's recovery? Booklist; BBYA (nominated 2007)

❑ Waid, Mark and others. *Superman: Birthright.* (2004) DC Comics, Illustrated. (1401202519). 304 pgs. Superman's origin, his early life, and his return to righting society's ills. The author maintains a faithful approach to the Superman story while bringing him back to a dramatic and dynamic existence. The author manages to incorporate some elements made popular by the television series featuring Clark Kent and Lois Lane in Smallville. Graphic Novel. BBYA (2006)

❑ Walker, Sally M. *Secrets of a Civil War Submarine: Solving the Mysteries of the H.L. Hunley.* (2005) Carolrhoda/Lerner. (1575058308). 112 pgs. The sinking and raising of the H.L. Hunley is augmented with photos, illustrations, and primary sources that document and provide a complete account of the submarine. VOYA Non-fiction

❑ Werlin, Nancy. *Rules of Survival.* (2006) Dial. (0803730012). 272 pgs. Written as a retrospective letter to his younger step-sister Emmy, this tale is one of frightening reality. Matthew must not only protect himself from the abuse of his psychotic mother but must help his sister Callie and Emmy from getting in the way of her rage as well. A distant father and an apathetic aunt are little help, but their mother's ex-boyfriend finds a way to become a change agent and create hope and a future for the three children. An inspired novel by a master storyteller. SLJ; Booklist; Kirkus; BCCB; BBYA (nominated 2007); Quick Picks (nominated 2007).

❑ Westerfeld, Scott. *Peeps.* (2005) Penguin/Razorbill. (159514031X). 320 pgs. A fantasy novel that has college freshman Cal coming to NY and spending a night with a beautiful girl. He becomes a carrier and now everyone he kisses develops a craving for meat, an aversion to sunlight, and super strength. Vampires, horror, but no gore. BCCB Blue Ribbon Fiction; BBYA (2006); SLJ

❑ Westerfeld, Scott. *Uglies.* (2005) Simon & Schuster/Simon Pulse. (0689865384). 441 pgs. Tally can't wait for her 16th birthday and the surgery that will transform her into a "pretty". Because if everyone is beautiful, everything is perfect— right? Additional books in the Uglies Trilogy include: *Pretties* (Book 2; 2005), *Specials* (Book 3; 2006) BBYA2006-Top10 BBYA (2006); BCCB; Booklist; SLJ

❑ Whitcomb, Laura. *A Certain Slant of Light.* (2005) Houghton/Graphia, (061858532X). 288 pgs. When a body is living but whose spirit within has died, it is open for inhabitation by a spirit that is living but whose body has died. And so that is how Helen, who died 130 years ago came to inhabit the body of Jenny, and James, who had died years earlier had come to inhabit the body of Billy. James's and Helen's romance includes both modern and old-fashioned events and is told in a story in which explicit sex is far from gratuitous or formulaic. BBYA (2006)

❑ Windsor, Patricia. **Nightwood**. (2006) Random House/Delacorte. (0385903316). 256 pgs. Three girls at a cabin, just across the lake from three boys on a fishing trip—a much better plan than going on the senior class trip. No parents, nobody to tell them what to do or when, no curfew, and nobody to help when the first body shows up. No one to save them when the knock comes on the door. A week in the woods will be much more horrifying than Casey, Gena, or Maryann could possibly imagine. BBYA (nominated 2007)

❑ Wittlinger, Ellen. **Sandpiper.** (2005) Simon & Schuster. (0689868022). 240 pgs. Sandpiper Hollow Ragsdale (15) is a promiscuous teen who engages in oral sex to satisfy her need to be needed. Derek, one of her rejected boys, harassed Piper and her family. When Piper hooks up in a platonic relationship with another teen, Aidan "Walker," one who is often seen roaming the roads of her small Massachusetts town, she finds a confidante and a friend who rescues her. A frank look at relationships and at the myth that oral sex really isn't sex. BBYA (2006)

❑ Wooding, Chris. **Poison**. (2005) Scholastic/Orchard. (0439755700). 288 pgs. Phaeries kidnap Poison's baby sister and leave a changeling in the baby's crib. Poison sets out to get her back but finds much more than she expects. BBYA2006-Top10 BBYA (2006); BCCB; Kirkus

❑ Wooding, Chris. **The Storm Thief**. (2006) Scholastic/Orchard. (0439865131). 320 pgs. The city of Orokos has stood undisturbed on a rocky island for centuries. No one living in the city even questions what lies beyond its walls. But when street thieves Rail and Moa steal an artifact, a golem of metal and flesh, and make a discovery that might change their society, the two are targeted by the most powerful citizens in the city. BBYA (nominated 2007)

❑ Wynne-Jones, Tim. **A Thief in the House of Memory**. (2005) Farrar/Melanie Kroupa. Illustrated. (0374374783). 224 pgs. Declan's mother died 10 years ago and many secrets surround his memories and her death. When a man is found dead in the old family home, it sets in motion efforts to learn those secrets from his mother's best friend and from his dad. A coming-of-age novel. BBYA (2006)

❑ Zenatti, Valérie. **When I Was a Soldier: A Memoir.** (2005) Bloomsbury. (1582349789). How being a soldier (during compulsory military service) made an adult of Valerie Zenatti, a French immigrant and Israeli citizen. Her life changes forever. Non-fiction; BBYA (2006); Booklist; BCCB; Mildred L. Batchelder Honor

❑ Zusak, Markus. **I Am the Messenger**. (2005) Knopf. (0375830995). 368 pgs. Ed Kennedy is a loser cab driver, 19-years-old, and no future in sight and then he foils a bank robbery. Soon after the robbery, he begins to receive coded messages on playing cards. The coded messages direct him onto life-altering missions—missions to help people and make changes in his own life. But who is sending the life-altering missions? And what is to become of it all? BBYA2006-Top10 BBYA (2006); BCCB; Booklist; PW; SLJ

Section 2

Top Titles
from 2003-05

A select list of books previously included in
Best Teen Reads 2005

The Best Teen Reads 2003-05—A Select List

❑ Adams, Lorraine. (2004) **Harbor.** Knopf. (140004233X) fiction; 304 pgs. After 52 days as a stowaway in a tanker's hold, Aziz swims to shore in the Boston Harbor. Aziz has successfully fled Algeria—but has trouble and the FBI followed him? PW; Kirkus

❑ Adichie, Chimamanda Ngozi. (2003) **Purple Hibiscus**. Algonquin Books of Chapel Hill. (1565123875) 320 pgs. Kambili's dysfunctional family begins to unravel during the political unrest in their Nigerian community. ALA Best Book—2004

❑ Alexander, Alma. (2004) **The Secrets of Jin-Shei**. HarperCollins. (0060563419). 512 pgs. A mythical Chinese realm where mothers pass to daughters the secret language of *jin-shei*. Friendships form across all classes because of the language and those friendships will change the fate of their world.

❑ Balliett, Blue. (2004) **Chasing Vermeer**. Illustrated by Brett Helquist. Scholastic. (0439372941). 272 pgs. When unexplained occurrences begin to happen, Petra Andalee and Calder Pillary know it will be up to them to solve the puzzle that is unfolding. Knowledge about the artist Vermeer takes center stage in this puzzle filled mystery novel.

❑ Bell, Hilari. (2003) **The Goblin Wood**. HarperCollins/Eos. (0060513713; 0060513721 lib) fiction; 304 pgs. A magical world: hedge witch, a knight, and a myriad of goblins. ALA Best Book—2004

❑ Bowler, Tim. (2003) **Firmament**. Simon & Schuster, McElderry Books. (0689861613) fiction; 320pg. The death of fourteen-year-old Luke's father gives him a lot to cope with, and when his new gang of "friends" begin to make demands, he must figure out how to deal with the bullies, a lonely old woman, a blind young girl, his mother's romantic involvement, and his own musical talent.

❑ Brooks, Kevin. (2004) **Kissing the Rain**. Scholastic/The Chicken House. (043957742X) fiction; 336 pgs. Moo Nelson often visits the bridge to get some peace and quiet—to get away from the verbal abuse he suffers daily. But one day the peace and tranquility of his bridge is disturbed—disturbed by what he witnesses from his high above the expressway vantage point. Booklist

❑ Bruchac, Joseph. (2004) **Hidden Roots**. Scholastic Press. (0439353580) fiction; 208 pgs. Eleven-year-old Sonny, a shy boy, faces his father's rage every day. His fragile mother is loving but not able to protect him. It is Sonny's Uncle Louis and a supportive librarian who help Sonny gain the confidence to face the family's hidden secrets and the truth about his Native-American roots. Upstate NY 1950s.

❑ Byrd, Robert. (2003) **Leonardo, Beautiful Dreamer**. Dutton. (0525470336) Biography; 40 pgs. Notes from Leonardo's notebooks. Detailed drawings showing his artistic and scientific endeavors. SJL Best Books 2004

❑ Carbone, Elisa. (2005) **Last Dance on Holladay Street**. Knopf/Random House. (0375828966 trd); 0375928960 lib) fiction; 208 pgs. Historical novel set in 1878 in Colorado. Thirteen-year-old Eva seeks her birth mother and finds out the city and her mother are not what she imagined.

- Choldenko, Gennifer. (2004) *Al Capone Does My Shorts*. Putnam. (0399238611) fiction. 228 pgs. Set in 1935 when guards lived on Alcatraz Island with their families. Moose Flannagan's dad is one of those prison guards. Moose's sister, Natalie, is autistic and must attend a special school, but the whole family deals with her care. When Moose meets the warden's daughter and she devises a scheme to make money from the other children on the island, Moose realizes that the issue is not just black and white. If he deals with Piper will he jeopardize his father's job? But if he doesn't will she find a way to impact the family's situation anyway? NEWBERY HONOR

- Creech, Sharon. (2004) *Heartbeat*. Joanna Cotler (06054022) fiction; 192 pgs. A tenderhearted story told in spare, free-verse poems. Annie, 12, takes great pleasure in running, but has no interest in racing or becoming a member of a team, but for Max it is a different story.

- Crowe, Chris. (2003) *Getting Away With Murder: The True Story of the Emmett Till Case*. Penguin Putnam/Phyllis Fogelman Books. (0803728042) non-fiction; 128 pgs. The murder of a 14-year-old black boy from Chicago touches off the Civil Rights Movement of the 1960s. ALA Best Book—2004; SJL Best Books 2004

- Crowley, Bridget. *Feast of Fools*. Margaret K. Elderry. (0689865120) fiction; 272 pgs. A medieval mystery. A young man injured in the accident that killed his father becomes an outcast and then forges a friendship with two others with a similar social stigma. Later he finds that it is up to him to protect his friends from the injustice they are about to face as suspects in a double murder. Nominee for Edgar YA mystery Award—2004

- Crutcher, Chris. (2003) **King of the Mild Frontier: An Ill-Advised Autobiography**. HarperCollins/Greenwillow Press (0060502495; 0060502509 lib) non-fiction; 272 pgs. The autobiography of Margaret A. Edwards award-winning author Chris Crutcher.

- DeFelice, Cynthia. (2004) *The Ghost of Cutler Creek*. Farrar, Straus and Giroux. (0374380589) fiction; 181 pgs. When she sees the ghost of a dog, Allie begins to suspect that the surly new boy in school and his father are running a puppy mill. MS

- DeFelice, Cynthia. (2005) *The Missing Manatee*. Farrar, Straus and Giroux. (03743312575) While coping with his parents' separation, eleven-year-old Skeet spends most of Spring Break in his skiff on a Florida river, where he finds a manatee shot to death and begins looking for the killer.

- Delman, Carmit. (2003) *Burnt Bread and Chutney: Growing up between Cultures: A Memoir of an Indian Jewish Girl*. One World/Ballantine. (0345445937) biography; 288 pgs. The author shares her story of coming of age. SLJ Adult Books for HS—2004

- Deuker, Carl. (2005) *Runner*. Houghton Mifflin (0618542981) fiction. Living with his alcoholic father on a broken-down sailboat on Puget Sound has been hard on seventeen-year-old Chance Taylor, but when his love of running leads to a high-paying job, he quickly learns that the money is not worth the risk.

❑ Dicamillo, Kate. (2003) *Tale of Despereaux: Being the Story of a Mouse, a Princess, Some Soup, and a Spool of Thread*. (0763617229) fiction; 272 pgs. A tiny mouse with huge ears, Despereaux, reads stories about knights, loves music, falls in love with a princess, and is sentenced to death for communicating with humans. A story filled with forgiveness, light, love, and soup. Newberry Award 2004

❑ Donnelly, Jennifer. (2003) *A Northern Light*. Harcourt. (0152167056) 400 pgs. An actual murder in Upstate New York (1906) is the backdrop for Mattie Gokey (a fictional character) and her emergence as her own person. ALA Best Book—2004; Michael A. Printz Honor 2004; SLJ Best Books 2004

❑ Draper, Sharon. *The Battle of Jericho*. Atheneum (0689842325) fiction: 304 pgs. The consequences of choices are the ultimate result of the initiation into the Ohio High School's elite club, The Warriors of Distinction. MS–HS CORETTA SCOTT KING HONOR 2004

❑ Dumas, Firoozeh. *Funny in Farsi: A Memoir of Growing up Iranian in America*. Villard. (1400060400) fiction; 208 pgs. Humorous tales describe Dumas's introduction to American culture. SLJ Adult Books for HS 2004

❑ Fleming, Candace. (2003) *Ben Franklin's Almanac: Being a True Account of the Good Gentleman's Life*. Simon & Schuster/Atheneum. (0689835493) non-fiction; 128 pgs. A topically organized biography modeled on Franklin's own Poor Richard's Almanac. ALA Best Book—2004; SLJ Best Books 2004

❑ Fradin, Dennis Brindell and Judith Bloom Fradin. (2003) *Fight On! Mary Church Terrell's Battle for Integration*. Houghton Mifflin Company/Clarion Books. (0618133496) biography; 192 pgs. In the late '80s Terrell conducted a successful campaign to integrate D.C. restaurants and movie theaters. ALA Best Book—2004

❑ Frank, E. R. (2003) *Friction: A Novel*. S & S/Atheneum/A Richard Jackson Book. (068985384X) fiction; 208 pgs. An innocent young girl's budding sexuality contributes to the tragic consequences when a new classmate rallies to portray their popular teacher as a pervert. ALA Best Book—2004

❑ Freedman, Russell. (2003) *In Defense of Liberty: The Story of America's Bill of Rights*. Holiday House. (0823415856) non-fiction; 196 pgs. Focuses on the Bill of Rights, the first ten amendments to the U.S. Constitution, ratified in 1791 and the changes over the years. ALA Best Book—2004; SLJ Best Books 2004

❑ Freedman, Russell. (2004) *Voice That Challenged a Nation: Marian Anderson and the Struggle for Equal Rights*. Clarion. (0618159762) 128 pgs. When the Daughters of the American Revolution refused to allow Anderson to sing in Constitution Hall, Eleanor Roosevelt brought her to the steps of the Lincoln Memorial and she sang for an audience of 75,000 people and a national radio audience. A significant event in the civil rights movement. Team with Pam Munoz Ryan's and Brian Selznick's stunningly beautiful 40-page picture book, *When Marian Sang*. (Scholastic Press, 2002) NEWBERY HONOR BOOK 2005; Robert F. Siebert Award 2005

❑ Frost, Helen. *Keesha's House*. Farrar, Straus & Giroux/Frances Foster Books. (0374340641) 138 pgs. Joe's aunt took him in as a youth and now he does the same for a variety of kids with their own problems. ALA Best Book—2004; Michael A. Printz Honor 2004

❑ Going, K. L. (2004) **Fat Kid Rules the World**. Penguin Putnam/G.P.Putnam's Sons. (0399239901) fiction; 187 pgs. Seventeen-year-old Troy is rescued from a near-suicide attempt by a chance encounter. ALA Best Book—2004; Michael A. Printz Honor 2004; SLJ Best Books 2004

❑ Gutman, Dan. **Abner & Me: A Baseball Card Adventure**. HarperCollins (0060534435; 0060534443 lib) fiction. With his ability to travel through time using baseball cards and photographs, thirteen-year-old Joe and his mother go back to 1863 to ask Abner Doubleday whether he invented baseball, but instead find themselves in the middle of the Battle of Gettysburg. A05 MS

❑ Haddon, Mark. **The Curious Incident of the Dog in the Night-Time: A Novel**. Random House/Doubleday. (0385509456) fiction; 240 pgs. Christopher is autistic and sees the world differently. It just might be the difference that helps him solve two mysteries: who killed the dog and what happened to his mother. (OSBCB, social studies—2004; SLJ Adult Books for HS 2004; ALA Best Book—2004) HS–Adult

❑ Hansen, Drew D. **The Dream: Martin Luther King Jr. and the Speech That Inspired a Nation**. HarperCollins. (0060084766) non-fiction; 304 pgs. Insight into King's life and his dream. Those interested in the moral issues tied to the civil rights struggle will enjoy Hansen's analysis. (OSBCB, History—2004) MS–HS

❑ Hautman, Pete. (2003) **Sweetblood**. Simon & Schuster. (0689850484) fiction; 192 pgs. As a way to cope with her diabetes, sixteen-year-old Lucy compares her disease to a blood-dependent vampire and immerses herself in Goth culture. ALA Best Book—2004

❑ Henkes, Kevin. (2003) **Olive's Ocean**. HarperCollins/Greenwillow Books. (0060535431; 006053544X lib) fiction; 224 pgs. When Olive is killed her classmate Martha, inspired by a letter from Olive's journal, takes up the torch for Olive's causes. ALA Best Book—2004

❑ Holt, Kimberly Willis. (2003) **Keeper of the Night**. Henry Holt and Company. (0805063617) fiction; 180 pgs. A Guam teenager tries to help her family survive after her mother's suicide. ALA Best Book—2004; SLJ Best Books 2004

❑ Holzer, Harold. (2003) **The President is Shot: The Assassination of Abraham Lincoln**. 144 pages, Boyds Mills Pr; (1563979853) non-fiction; 144 pgs. America's foremost expert on the Civil War and Lincoln presents a fascinating array of photos and archival illustrations, and an event that changed the course of history.

❑ Horvath, Polly. (2003) **The Canning Season**. Farrar, Straus & Giroux. (0374399565) fiction; 208 pgs. When her mother ships her off to spend the summer with her twin aunts, the last thing Ratchet Clark expects to find is a real home. ALA Best Book—2004; SLJ Best Books 2004; National Book Award for Young People's Literature.

❑ Hosseini, Khaled. (2003) **The Kite Runner**. Putman/Riverhead. (1573222453) fiction; 324 pgs. Amir returns to Afghanistan to make amends for betraying his best friend before he fled Kabul and the Taliban. OSBCB, social studies—2004, Alex Award, SLJ Adult Books for HS 2004

❑ Janeczko, Paul, editor. (2005) **A Kick in the Head**. Illustrated by Chris Raschka. Candlewick Press (0763606626) poetry. No blurb but anything Janeczko does is usually great. Picture book format

❑ Johnson, Angela. (2003) *The First Part Last*. Simon & Schuster Books for Young Readers. (0689849222) fiction; 144 pgs. Continues the story of Bobby Morris (*Heaven*, 1998), a teenage father, who is raising his daughter Feather. ALA Best Book—2004; Michael A. Printz Award 2004) MS–HS

❑ Kadohata, Cynthia. (2004) *Kira-Kira*. Atheneum Books for Young Readers. (0689856393) fiction; 256 pgs. When one sister becomes terminally ill, the close friendship between two Japanese-American sisters growing up in rural Georgia during the late 1950s and early 1960s is both their strength and their sadness. NEWBERY AWARD 2005

❑ Kimmel, Eric A, author and compiler. (2003) *Wonders and Miracles: A Passover Companion*. Illustrated with art spanning 3,000 years. (0439071755). Scholastic Press; 144 pgs. A compilation of traditions surrounding the Passover holiday the world over. (Starred Kirkus, January 2004; Starred SLJ, February 2004) All ages.

❑ Konigsburg, E. L. (2004) *The Outcasts of 19 Schuyler Place*. Atheneum Books for Young Readers. (0689866364) fiction; 304 pgs. When the three unique towers that her grand uncles have been building in their back yard for over forty years are threatened, twelve-year-old Mary Rose Kane organizes a campaign to help save them.

❑ Korman, Gordon. (2004) *Son of the Mob: Hollywood Hustle*. Hyperion. (0786809183) fiction; 213 pgs. Vince Luca, the son of a mob boss, elects a college in California in order to escape his past. But his past, his brother and several of his "uncles," show up at his dorm and soon he is back in the criminal fold once again.

❑ Krisher, Trudy. (2003) *Uncommon Faith*. Holiday House. (0823417913) fiction; 263 pgs.

Young people in 1837 Millbrook, Massachusetts protest the establishment's treatment of women and slaves. (ALA Best Book—2004)

❑ Levithan, David. (2003) *Boy Meets Boy*. Random House/Alfred A. Knopf. (0375824006; 0375924000 lib) fiction; 192 pgs. Paul "Gay Boy" is torn between his friend Kyle and a new acquaintance, Noah. ALA Best Book—2004; BCCB Blue Ribbon Fiction Book Award

❑ Lowry, Lois. (2004) *Messenger*. Houghton Mifflin/Walter Lorrajne Books for Young Readers. (0689851685) fiction; 304 pgs. Set in a small Alabama town in 1947–1956. When Sonny's father packs up and leaves, the family's situation changes immensely. This is a coming-of-age novel with references to family, religion, racial prejudice, and homosexuality.

❑ Mackler, Carolyn. (2004) *The Earth, My Butt, and Other Big Round Things*. Candlewick Press. (0763619582) fiction; 256 pgs. Fifteen-year-old Virginia deals with her weight and several obstacles as she learns to be on her own for the first time. ALA Best Book—2004; Michael A. Printz Honor 2004

❑ Manning, Sarra. (2004) *Guitar Girl*. Dutton. (0525472347) fiction; 256 pgs. Sex, drugs, and music. Molly and her girlfriends form a band, "The Hormones." When a couple of older boys smooze their way into the band they begin to get big gigs, an American tour, and lots of fame, but success is not free and Molly is about to find out just what it costs. National Council for the Social Studies, 2004

❑ Martinez, Manuel Luis. (2003) *Drift: A Novel*. St. Martin's Press/Picador. (0312309953 pbk) fiction; 256 pgs. It is his Grams who helps sixteen-year-old Robert face his family demons and get his own life together. ALA Best Book—2004

❑ Mazer, Harry. (2005) **Heroes Don't Run: A Novel of the Pacific War**. Simon & Schuster Books for Young Readers (0689855346) fiction. To honor his father who died during the Japanese invasion of Pearl Harbor, seventeen-year-old Adam eagerly enlists in the Marines in 1944, survives boot camp, and faces combat on the tiny island of Okinawa.

❑ McKissack, Patricia C. and Fredrick L. McKissack. (2003) **Days of Jubilee: The End of Slavery in the United States**. Illustrated by Leo Dillon and Diane Dillon. Scholastic. (059010764X) non-fiction; 144 pgs. There was not just one day that freed all slaves—from the end of the Revolution when many African-Americans who had served with the patriot army to the Emancipation Proclamation there were many days for various slaves or slave groups, Days of Jubilee when they became free. CORETTA SCOTT KING AWARD 2004

❑ McNamee, Graham. **Acceleration**. Random House Children's Books/Wendy Lamb (0385731191, 0385901445 lib) fiction; 224 pgs. Duncan discovers a lost journal containing a man's plans to murder women. ALA Best Book—2004; Nominee for Edgar YA mystery Award—2004; VOYA Top Ten

❑ Moriarty, Jaclyn. **The Year of Secret Assignments**. Arthur A. Levine Books. (0439498813) fiction; 352 pgs. A sequel to *Feeling Sorry for Celia*. Three friends, Lydia, Emily, and Cassie are all assigned male pen pals at rival Brookfield high. But the letter writing is not so simple. Before the exchange is over there is much havoc, humor, and all-out war between the schools. Booklist

❑ Morris, Dave & Leo Hartas. **Game Art: The Graphic Art of Computer Games**. Watson-Guptill. (0823020800) non-fiction; 192 pages. A visual feast for serious or casual gamers. SLJ Adult Books for HS 2004

❑ Morrison, Toni. (2004) **Remember: The Journey to School Integration**. (061839740X) fiction; 80 pgs. Filled with archival photographs depicting historical events surrounding school desegregation integrate with a fictional account of the dialogue and emotions of the children who lived during the era of "separate but equal" schooling. CORETTA SCOTT KING AWARD 2005

❑ Moses, Shelia P. (2004) **The Legend of Buddy Bush**. (0689858396) fiction. 224 pgs. Set in 1947, Uncle Buddy returns home to North Carolina. Uncle Buddy doesn't pay enough attention to the protocol of the times and ends up in jail for a crime against a white woman. Pattie Mae's life is destined to change. CORETTA SCOTT KING AWARD 2005

❑ Murphy, Jim. (2003) **An American Plague: The True and Terrifying Story of the Yellow Fever Epidemic of 1793**. Houghton Mifflin Company/Clarion. (0395776082) non-fiction; 192 pgs. Thousands of lives in Philadelphia were lost in the disastrous epidemic of 1793. A tribute to the African-American community who saved many lives. ALA Best Book—2004; SLJ Best Books 2004; Newbery Honor—2004

❑ Murphy, Jim. (2003) **Inside the Alamo**. Random House, Inc./Delacorte Press (0385325746; 0385900929 lib) non-fiction; 121 pgs. Recounts the battle in February 1836 when Santa Anna led to Mexican Army to reclaim the Alamo for Mexico. ALA Best Book—2004

❑ Myers, Walter Dean. (2004) **Shooter**. Amistad. (0060295198; 0060295201 lib) fiction; 224 pgs. Written in the form of interviews, reports, and journal entries, the story of three troubled teenagers ends in a tragic school shooting. A04 MS–HS

❑ Myers, Walter Dean. (2004) **USS Constellation: Pride of the American Navy**. Holiday House (0823418162) non-ficton. 96 pgs. Tall and majestic, the U.S.S. Constellation (restored and now in Baltimore) was in America's first naval fleet. Myers documents its travels, from its heroic role in patrolling and intercepting ships used in the illegal African slave trade to its exploits in the Civil War protecting the Union and defeating Confederate vessels. Historical drawings and photographs, chronology, glossary, index.

❑ Nelson, Marilyn. (2004) **Fortune's Bones: The Manumission Requiem**. Front Street. (1932425128) poetry; 32 pgs. A skeleton of a slave has been in the Mattatuck Museum in Waterbury, Connecticut for over 200 years. This poem is in honor of Fortune, the slave, and his life. CORETTA SCOTT KING HONOR AWARD 2005.

❑ Oppel, Keith. (2004) **Airborn**. Eos. (0060531800); fiction; 368 pgs. Matt, a fifteen-year-old, is a cabin boy about a luxurious airship. When Kate and her chaperone come aboard Kate is determined to verify her grandfather's claims of having seen strange creature flying in the sky. A lively science fiction. BCCB Blue Ribbon Book; PRINTZ HONOR AWARD 2005.

❑ Parker, Jeff. (2003) **The Interman**. Octopus. (0972555307) graphic novel, fiction; 128 pgs. Van Meach is the Interman. His secret project for the government makes him a valuable employee and a dangerous employee. (ALA Best Book—2004)

❑ Paulsen, Gary. (2003) **How Angel Peterson Got His Name: And Other Outrageous Tales About Extreme Sports**. Random House Children's Books/ Wendy Lamb Books. (0385729499) non-fiction; 128 pgs. Gary Paulsen relates a series of bizarre and daredevil feats from his childhood in Minnesota. ALA Best Book—2004

❑ Paulsen, Gary. (2004) **The Quilt**. Random House Children's Books/ Wendy Lamb Books. (0385729502) non-fiction; 128 pgs. Set in 1944 a six-year-old boy goes to live with his grandmother Alida in a small town close to the Canadian border. He learns about family support when his cousin is about to give birth.

❑ Peck, Richard. (2003) **The River Between Us**. Penguin Putnam/Dial. (0803727356) fiction; 164 pgs. A family's involvement in the Civil War as told in 1916 to Howard Leland Hutchings. ALA Best Book—2004

❑ Philbrick, Rodman. (2004) **The Young Man and the Sea**. Scholastic/The Blue Sky Press. (0439368294) fiction; 192 pgs. Skiff Beaman is determined to take care of his family despite overwhelming odds. If his father can't, he will.

❑ Pringle, Peter. (2003) **Food, Inc.: Mendel to Monsanto—The Promises and Perils of the Biotech Harvest**. Simon & Schuster. (0743226119) nonfiction; 356 pgs. Complexities of genetic science, academic politics, and corporate strategies are discussed. SLJ Adult Books for HS 2004

❑ Rector, Anne Elizabeth with Kathleen Krull. (2004) **Anne Elizabeth's Diary: A Young Artist's True Story**. Megan Tigley/Little Brown. (0316072044) biography; 64 pgs. The diary of a twelve-year-old girl living in New York City in 1912, with sidebars describing the author/illustrator's life and family and significant events of the year and the city.

❏ Roach, Mary. (2003) *Stiff: The Curious Lives of Human Cadavers*. W.W. Norton & Company, Inc. (0393050939) non-fiction; 224 pgs. A respectful and poignant look at how scientists utilize every precious element of the human body. ALA Best Book—2004; OSBCB, science—2004; SLJ Adult Books for HS 2004

❏ Robinson, Sharon. (2003) *Promises to Keep: How Jackie Robinson Changed America*. Scholastic Press. (0439425921) non-fiction; 64 pgs. The only daughter of the man who broke the color barrier in major league baseball tells of his hard-won victories in baseball, business, politics, and civil rights. Booklist

❏ Rosoff, Meg. *how i live now*. Wendy Lamb/Random House. (0385746776) fiction; 208 pgs. Daisy (15) is sent to England to live. When war breaks out Daisy, She finds herself with her cousins without adult supervision. Daisy and her cousin Edmond fall in love but then are separated during the occupation. Their psychic connection continues until an unspeakable event breaks that connection. PRINTZ AWARD BOOK 2005

❏ Rowling, J.K. (2003) *Harry Potter and the Order of the Phoenix*. Mary Grandpre, illustrator. Scholastic, Inc. (043935806X, 0439567610 lib) fiction; 870 pgs. Harry Potter is haunted by dreams that foreshadow a terrifying secret. This volume approaches Harry's coming-of-age. ALA Best Book—2004

❏ Satrapi, Marjane. (2003) *Persepolis: The Story of a Childhood*. Random House, Inc./Pantheon. (0375422307) non-fiction; 160 pgs. Marjane, the daughter of radical Marxists, grows up in Iran during the time of its revolution and subsequent war. ALA Best Book—

2004; SLJ Adult Books for HS 2004; Alex Awards

❏ Schmidt, Gary D. (2004) *Lizzie Bright and the Buckminster Boy*. Clarion (0618439293) historical fiction; 224 pgs. The elders in Phippsburg, Maine frown upon the minister's son's friendship with Lizzie, a resident of the island they want to destroy. The island, settled years ago by African-Americans (former or escaped slaves), is slated to be destroyed to make way for the town's planned tourist village. NEWBERY HONOR AWARD 2005; PRINTZ HONOR AWARD 2005

❏ Shoup, Barbara. (2003) *Vermeer's Daughter*. Guild. (1578601312) fiction; 150 pgs. The compelling tale of the artist Vermeer's household as told by the fictional daughter of the Dutch painter. SLJ Adult Books for HS 2004

❏ Simon, Rachel. (2003) *Riding the Bus with My Sister: A True Life Journey*. Houghton. (0618045996) non-fiction: 256 pgs. Tagging along with her mentally retarded sister on her daily travels, she learns much about her sister and other travelers. SLJ Adult Books for HS 2004

❏ Sis, Peter. (2003) *The Tree of Life: A Book Depicting the Life of Charles Darwin: Naturalist, Geologist & Thinker*. Farrar, Straus, Giroux/Frances Foster. (0374456283) non-fiction; 44 pgs. An introduction to the nineteenth century scientist who sailed around the world and wrote a book that changed it. ALA Best Book—2004

❏ Spinelli, Jerry. (2003) *Milkweed: A Novel*. Random House, Inc./Alfred A. Knopf. (0375813748; 0375913742 lib) fiction; 224 pgs. An orphan struggles to survive the horrors of the Warsaw ghetto in Nazi-occupied Poland. ALA Best Book—2004; Golden Kite Award

- Starkey, David. (2003) *Six Wives: The Queens of Henry VIII*. HarperCollins. (069401043X; 0060005505 pb) non-fiction; 880 pgs. One man's marriages that changed structure of power in a nation and shook the foundations of the Catholic Church. OSBCB, History—2004

- Stratton, Allan. (2004) *Chanda's Secrets*. Annick Press. (1550378341) fiction; 176 pgs. Chanda remembers a time when her family's situation was relatively good. But when her father is killed in a diamond mine, the family's situation turns. Her third step-father is a drunken philanderer and succeeds in infecting Chanda's mother with AIDS. Chanda finds herself figuring out how to keep the family intact and make a future for herself and her siblings. Set in sub-Saharan Africa. PRINTZ HONOR AWARD 2005.

- Trueman, Terry. (2003) *Inside Out*. HarperCollins/HarperTempest. (0066239621; 006623963X lib) fiction; 128 pgs. Sixteen-year-old Zach, suffering from adolescent onset schizophrenia, helps to diffuse a hostage situation after a foiled bank robbery by two armed teens. ALA Best Book—2004

- Von Drehle, David. (2003) *Triangle: The Fire That Changed America*. Atlantic Monthly Press. non-fiction; 352 pgs. An event that changed the lives of working people everywhere. OSBCB, History—2004

- Werlin, Nancy. (2004) *Double Helix*. Dial Books. (0803726066) fiction; 252 pgs. Eighteen-year-old Eli can sense that his parents have a secret, but only when he goes to work for a Nobel Prize-winning genetic scientist does Eli found out the shocking secret.

- Winspear, Jacqueline. (2003) *Maisie Dobbs*. Soho. (1569473307) fiction; 336 pgs. A serving girl gives up the opportunity for a Cambridge education to serve as a nurse during World War I. A mix of mystery, war story and romance set in WWI-era England. SLJ Adult Books for HS 2004; Alex Awards

- Wittlinger, Ellen. (2003) *Zigzag*. Simon & Schuster. (0689849966) fiction; 227 pgs. Robin discovers more than the sights during her cross-country trek with her Aunt Dory and her two younger cousins. A right-of-passage journey. ALA Best Book—2004

- Woodson, Jacqueline. (2003) *Locomotion*. Penguin Putnam/G.P. Putnam's Sons. (0399231153) fiction; 128 pgs. A verse novel in which 11-year-old Lonnie recovers from the trauma that results when his parents are killed in a fire. ALA Best Book—2004; CORETTA SCOTT KING HONOR 2004

- Wrede, Patricia C. and Caroline Stevermer. (2003) *Sorcery & Cecelia, Or, The Enchanted Chocolate Pot: Being the Correspondence of Two Young Ladies of Quality Regarding Various Magical Scandals in London and the Country*. Harcourt, Inc. (0152046151) fiction; 336 pgs. Correspondence between Cousins Cecelia and Kate records Kate's first season in London. ALA Best Book—2004; VOYA Top Ten

- Yolen, Jane. (2003) *Sword of the Rightful King: A Novel of King Arthur*. Harcourt, Inc. (0152025278) fiction; 368 pgs. King Arthur's early days of rule, including the magician's very risky staging of the test of the sword in the stone. ALA Best Book—2004

- Zahn, Timothy. (2003) *Dragon and Thief: A Dragonback Adventure*. Tom Doherty Associates/Tor. (0765301245; 0765342723 pb) fiction; 256 pgs. Jack Morgan's efforts to be cleared of a theft become complicated when a symbiotic dragon takes up residence on his back. ALA Best Book—2004

Section 3

Graphic Novels

Graphic Novels
Introduction

Graphic novels have arrived. After decades of existence, the graphic novel form is the fastest growing new category of publishing. In 2002 when *People Magazine* reviewed Doug TenNapel's *Creature Tech* (Top Shelf Productions), the magazine said, "TenNapel may be Generation X's answer to Dr. Seuss." Despite their existence, the mainstream culture continues to be slow to embrace the format, despite the Japanese invasion of Magna which lures young readers in such numbers that the format can no longer be ignored. In 2005 when one high school English teacher, who had just become acquainted with the format through a young adult literature class, came across a *People Magazine* book review of *Gemma Bovery* by Posy Simmonds (Pantheon, 2005), she said, "A few weeks ago I had not noticed graphic novels and now, here they are in the mainstream adult reading."

Another teacher, who had a heightened awareness for the format, noticed an article in *English Journal* ("Bold Books for Innovative Teaching" by Stephen Weiner [November 2004, 94:2, p. 114). Weiner said, "Well-done graphic novels offer teachers another tool to be used in the classroom ... enticing reluctant readers...." That teacher took notice as well.

Graphic novels are the ultimate in "show don't tell" writing.

If you are trying to decide whether or not to include graphic novels in your classroom or library, don't miss reading the speech "Graphic Novels in the Library: An Expert's Opinion," by Kathy Foster, University of North Texas History and Ethnography of Youth Information Services, available online at http://courses.unt.edu/efiga/HistoryAndEthnography/TrendsProjects/foster/FosterTrends.htm

Trends in graphic novels and what is to come are discussed in an article by Randy Dotinga, "'Tweens' Curl Up with Graphic Novels." in *Christian Science Monitor*. (2006 August 16) 98:183, p. 16-7.

For even more information check out some of the following references:

Books:

101 Best Graphic Novels by Steve Wiener (NBM Publishing Company, 2005 REVISED)

Getting Graphic! Using Graphic Novels to Promote Literacy with Preteens and Teens by Michele Gorman (Linworth, 2003)

Graphic Novels 101 Selecting and Using Graphic Novels to Promote Literacy for Children and Young Adults by Philip Charles Crawford (Hi Willow, 2003)

No Flying, No Tights: A Website Reviewing Graphic Novels for Teens. By Robin Brenner. http://www.noflyingnotights.com/

Online sites:

The Comics Get Serious: Graphic Novel Reviews and Other Stuff by D. Aviva Rothschild: http://www.rationalmagic.com/Comics/Comics.html

Comic Books for Young Adults: A Guide for Librarians Ed. by Michael R. Lavin: http://ublib.buffalo.edu/lml/comics/pages/

Graphic Novels and Books: http://www.indyworld.com/ic/amazon_catalog.html

Reviews of Graphic Novels/Diamond bookshelf:
http://bookshelf.diamondcomics.com/reviews/

Of special note is **The Librarian's Guide to Anime and Manga** by Gilles Poitras.
http://www.koyagi.com/Libguide.html

This site is mounted by Gilles Poitras, author of *The Anime Companion: What's Japanese in Japanese Animation* (Stone Bridge Press; ISBN 1880656329) and *Anime Essentials: Every Thing a Fan Needs to Know* (Stone Bridge Press; ISBN 1880656531).

He says that it is his "intent to promote the knowledge of Japanese culture as shown in popular entertainment from that country. ... and to produce online works of use to those who are curious about Japan through reading manga or watching anime."

A favorite Anime Magazine:
Anime Insider from Wizard Entertainment
http://www.wizarduniverse.com/ — click on "scriptions" and you will go to a page where one can subscribe to a number of magazines, including *Anime Insider*. 6 issues per year $18.00
WARNING: If students type in their search words "animeinsider" in the location box of a browser they will be taken to www.animeinsider.com—AN UNRECOMMENDED SITE

Links to Professional sites (Brodart):
> http://www.graphicnovels.brodart.com/links.htm

Graphic novels are one of the most effective formats for attracting reluctant readers. In the following section we have highlighted specific graphic titles that warrant your perusal and review. These titles will help with all types of readers.

Graphic Novels

❑ Abel, Jessica. *La Perdida*. (2006) Random House/ Pantheon Graphic Novels. (0375423656). Carla Olivares is a Mexican-American who decides to visit Mexico despite the fact that she cannot speak any Spanish. What she finds is a life in Mexico that she had not envisioned.

❑ Asakura, George. *A Perfect Day for Love Letters, Volume 2.* (2005) Ballantine Books/ Del Rey. (0345482670). Six short stories of teenage love. Letters, faxes, journals, and even popsicle sticks help in expressing that love.

❑ Axe, David and Steve Olexa, *War Fix*. (2006) NBM Publishing. (1561634638). 96 pgs. David Axe tells the story of his coverage in the Iraq war and his perceptions of the events surround the elections in Iraq as well as the fighting.

❑ Baker, Kyle. *Plastic Man Volume 2: Rubber Bandits*. (2006) DC Comics. (1401207294). Plastic Man is back in this collection of issues as he deals with homeland security, vampires, music piracy, and an evil mouse.

❑ Baum, L. Frank. *Puffin Graphics: Wizard of Oz*. (2005) Penguin Puffin Graphics. (0142404713). A Kansas farm girl dreams of adventure and gets caught in a tornado on the way to the Land of OZ.

❑ Bendis, Brian Michael. *House of M*. (2006) Marvel Enterprises. (0785117210). The X-Men and New Avengers all have what they wish for due to the powers of Wanda Maximoff, the Scarlett Witch, Wolverine is working to make changes to make things right.

❑ Burns, Charles. *Black Hole*. (2005) Random House/ Pantheon Graphic Novels. (037542380X). The setting is 1970 in Seattle and a plague is affecting teenagers throughout the city.

❑ Card, Orson Scott. *Ultimate Iron Man Volume 1*. (2006) Premiere HC. Marvel Enterprises. (078512151X). Because of a lab accident, Tony Stark, the son of an inventor and geneticist, was born a supergenius. Then greed destroyed everything and Tony and his father must strive for a normal life while on the run— avoiding evil forces that would harm them. This story tells of the childhood of Tony Stark, Iron Man.

❑ Carey, Mike. *Spellbinders: Signs and Wonders Digest*. (2005) Marvel Enterprises. (0785117563). 144 pgs. This volume collects Spellbinders volumes 1–6 of the episodes involving Kim Vesco, who moves from Chicago to Salem Massachusetts where she is caught between the two factions at the local school—the witches and the non-witches. Both sides are vying for her loyalty, but there seems to be other forces that want her dead. How will she keep herself from getting caught in the middle? How will she fight an enemy whose true identify has not been revealed?

❑ Chan, Queenie, Illustrator. *The Dreaming*. (2005) TOKYOPOP. (1598163825). An Australian boarding school becomes the home for twin sisters and their aunt who is teaching at the school. Their aunt instructs the girls to deny they are twins and to only say they are sisters. But then their aunt goes away, the sisters begin to have identical nightmares. When some of the other students begin to disappear their stay at the boarding school begins to take on a dark edge. A first in a series.

❑ Chmakova, Svetlana. *Dramacon.* (2005) TOKYOPOP. (1598161296). Set at an Anime/Manga Convention. Derek, Chris's boyfriend, seems to take her for granted, but she has made connections with dark and mysterious Matt. Chris and Derek engage in hi-jinks among the hotel rooms and convention floors while others sell their homemade comics. The illustrator has managed to use the international visual manga form to give a story that has emotion, humor, and a convincing storyline.

❑ Clamp. *Tsubasa 8: Reservoir Chronicle.* (2006) Ballantine Books/ Del Rey. (0345484282). 208 pgs. Five friends embark on a journey through alternate worlds searching for memories of Princess Sakura. The memories have been transformed into powerful magic feathers and those who possess them refuse to relinquish them. The friends are split and each group finds themselves in a conflict that threatens to destroy the young women performers.

❑ Clugston, Chynna. *Queen Bee.* (2005) ScholasticGraphix. (0439715725). Haley and Alexa each are able to use their psychokinetic powers to move objects with their minds. Each arrives at the same middle school as the and each wishes to be the "Queen Bee." Once the competition begins, middle school will never be the same. Readers will delight in the unpredictable mystery swirling around the girls who look alike.

❑ Crane, Jordan. *The Clouds Above.* (2005) Fantagraphics Books, 2005. (1560976276). On the way to school a boy and his cat take alternate routes—and end up traveling to different worlds.

❑ Delisle, Guy. *Pyongyang: A Journey in North Korea.* (2005) Drawn and Quarterly. (1896597890). A Canadian born animator travels to Japan when his company lands a big contract— these are his experiences in North Korea.

❑ Doyle, Arthur Conan. *Graphic Classics: Arthur Conan Doyle.* (2005) Eureka Productions/Graphic Classics. (0974664855). A collection of Arthur Conan Doyle's stories and poems put into graphic novel format.

❑ Eiichiro, Oda. *One Piece, Volume 11.* (2006) VIZ Media. (1421506637). Now up to 11 volumes this series was begun in 1997 and are now being translated into English. The series features Luffy, who became a pirate after listening to the tales of Shanks, a "red-haired" buccaneer. Now Luffy is in search of "One Piece," the greatest treasure in the world.

❑ Fies, Brian. *Mom's Cancer.* (2006) Abrams Image. (0810958406). Throughout his mother's Stage 4 lung/brain cancer, the author kept a running diary of the family's experience. At first the account was posted anonymously online and spread through word of mouth. Once in printed form the diary was awarded the first ever Eisner Award for Best Digital Comic.

❑ Ganter, Amy Kim. *Sorcerers and Secretaries.* (2006) TOKYOPOP. (1598164090). Nicole is a university student and part-time secretary but lives a life of loneliness. Josh is a player and has a jar full of love-notes. The bad boy falls for the "good" girl but the "good" girl's life is filled with fairytales.

❑ Gownley, Jimmy. *Amelia Rules! Book 3: Super Heroes.* (2005) ibooksipicturebooks. (1596878304). Amelia and Reggie (best friends) are looking forward to a long and exciting summer. Amelia's parents are still divorced and she and her mother live with her ex-rock star aunt.

❏ Grillo-Marxuach, Javier. *The Middleman: The Trade Paperback Imperative*. (2006) Viper Comics. (0975419374). Wendy Watson is the perfect partner for the Middle Man, a superhero who fights off the unknown and the supernatural using punches, wit, and an unstoppable sense of humor.

❏ Heinberg, Allan. *Young Avengers Volume 1: Sidekicks*. (2005) Marvel Enterprises. (078511470X). With the Avengers breaking up and leaving New York City, there is room for a group of young and heroic teens to come into the city as a new team to help fight evil. Before long the Young Avengers are faced with a battle with the most powerful villains in the history of the Avengers.

❏ Holm, Jennifer. *Babymouse: Our Hero*. (2005) Random House/Books for Young Readers. (0375832300). A typical little mouse, Babymouse does not like to get up for school. She daydreams during math class and always forgets her shoes on gym day. Wilson, the weasel, is her best friend and a cat named Felicia Furrypants is her archenemy.

❏ Johnson, R. Kikuo. *Night Fisher*. (2005) Fantagraphics Books. (1560977191). Loren's father works all the time and he and his best friend have drifted away. Getting high and committing petty crimes seem to get them back together again.

❏ Katayama, Kyoichi. *Socrates in Love: Volume One*. (2005) VIZ Media/Shojo Beat Manga. (1421501996). Two young lovers face the perils involved in dealing with leukemia.

❏ Kawai, Chigusa. *La Esperanca, Volume 1*. (2005) Digital Manga Publishers. (1569709335). Set in a European school dorm, George Saphir has loyal admirers. He does not allow anyone to get too close—until Robere comes into the picture.

Will letting Robere come closer lead to tragedy? Will the closeness bring George's worse fears to reality?

❏ Kibuishi, Kazu. *Flight, Vol. 3*. (2006) Ballantine Books/Del Rey, (0345490398). An anthology of monsters, magic, and mayhem by various authors.

❏ Kneese, Mark. *Trailers*. (2005) NBM Publishing. (1561634417). Forced to bury his mother's abusive boyfriend, Josh is haunted by nightmares that has his father returning. Josh's new girlfriend is scared of him and he still has to care for his siblings. If the situation continues, Josh feels that he will lose his sanity.

❏ Kyle, Craig. *X-23: Innocence Lost*. (2006) Marvel Enterprises. (0785115021). X-23 is unstoppable: cloned from Wolverine's DNA and raised in seclusion, he is trained to be an assassin for hire.

❏ Lash, Batton. *Tales of Supernatural Law*. (2005) Exhibit A Press. (0963395491). A collection of previously out-of-print tales of Alanna Wolff and Jeff Byrd, Counselors of the Macabre. These two attorneys represent human and supernatural clients. Familiar tales are intertwined with the representation given by Wolff and Byrd, including "The Monkey's Paw." Watch for a comic book cameo by Young Adult author Neil Gaiman.

❏ Lijewski, Christy. *RE:Play*. (2006) TOKYOPOP. (1598167375). Cree's band loses its bass player and needs to find another one. They feel lucky to have found Izsak who seems to be an excellent bass player. But shortly they begin to notice that the band is being stalked, and Izsak seems to have a strange and unknown past.

❏ Loeb, Jeph. *Catwoman: When in Rome*. (2005) DC Comics. (1401204325). Too much wrangling with Batman sends Selina Kyle, a.k.a. Catwoman, off to Rome to investigate her own family's past.

❏ Loeb, Jeph. ***Absolute Batman: Hush***. (2005) DC Comics. (1401204260). Poison Ivy, Joker and Harley Quinn face their own foe, the Dark Knight. And who among the knight's "allies"—Superman, Nightwing and Robin, Huntress, Catwoman—can he trust with Hush out for revenge?

❏ Martin, Ann M. ***Baby Sitter's Club: Kristy's Great Idea***. (2006) Scholastic Graphix. (0439802415). The story that began the Baby Sitter's Club is reborn as a graphic novel. Great illustrations.

❏ Matsushita, Yoko. ***Descendants of Darkness, Volume 9***. (2006) VIZ Media. (1421501716). The evil Dr. Muraki has had a showdown with his archenemy, the Shinigami partners Tsuzuki and Hisoka. But Hisoka, tired of the haggling, has decided to go on his own.

❏ McKeever, Sean. ***Mary Jane, Volume 2: Homecoming***. (2005) Marvel Enterprises. (0785117792). After her failed relationship with Spider Man, Mary Jane plans to go to homecoming with Harry Osburn. But soon she is accused of cheating on Harry with Flash Thompson.

❏ Medley, Linda. ***Castle Waiting***. (2006) Fantagraphics Books. (1560977477). A graphic version of the familiar Briar Rose fairy tale.

❏ Meltzer, Brad. ***Identity Crisis***. (2005) DC Comics. (1401206883). Secrets revealed cause problems with the hero's family and compromises their safety. When dirty secrets are uncovered the DC Universe goes into chaos.

❏ Moore, Alan. ***Watchmen: Absolute Edition***. (2005) DC Comics. (1401207138). The entire collection of the 12 issues of *Watchmen* in full color. Features the Crimebusters and a plot to kill them propel the story forward while the Watchmen explore the issues of power and control.

❏ Moore, Alan. ***V for Vendetta***. (2005) DC Comics. (1401207928). An alternative history tale set in England in 1997 where fascism and anarchy reign.

❏ Moore, Alan. ***Top Ten: 49'Ers***. (2006) DC Comics/Wildstorm Signature Series. (1401205739). A prequel to the popular Top Ten series. The skies of Neopolis are patrolled by the superhero police force, and this tale sets the stage for how that all came about. Set shortly after World War II, the super-heroes learn to adjust to another life.

❏ Murakami, Maki. ***Kimi No Unaji ni Kanpai!: Volume 1***. (2005) TOKYOPOP. (1595323171). Yamada Shintaro enrolls in the Taino Municipal Middle School hoping to finish his Monster guardian training. When he meets Nao, a beautiful reserved girl, he finds himself in love. But as part of his guardian training he must not possess any personal desires. Must he give up his love or his training?

❏ Naifeh, Ted. ***Unearthly***. (2005) Seven Seas Entertainment. (1933164093). Identity thief breaks up a traditional tale of a love triangle: the popular girl in school, a shy bookworm, and a random guy.

❏ Natsuki, Takaya. ***Fruits Basket, Vol. 12***. (2005) TOKYOPOP. (1595324070). This twelfth volume has Tohru visiting her grandfather while Yuki faces a new foe and Kyo's time is spent being mad. All return to school, including Shigure, who is not eager for the teacher/parent conferences.

❏ Nibot, Root. ***Banana Sunday***. (2006) Oni Press. (1932664378). Kirby and her three talking monkeys find it difficult to fit into the new school. But Kirby does seem to find new friends in Nickel, a school news reporter who is interested in finding out the real story behind the talking monkeys; and in Martin who is just interested in her for herself.

❑ Ohba, Tsugumi. **Death Note: Volume 2.** (2005) VIZ Media. (1421501694). When one of Shinigami's "Death Notes" is put into someone's name that person is dead within 40 hours. When one of Shinigami's noes are accidentally dropped into the human world it is found by Light, an honor high school student.

❑ Ottaviani, Jim. **Bone Sharps, Cowboys, and Thunder Lizards: Edward Drinker Cope, Othniel Charles Marsh, and the Gilded Age of Paleontology**. (2005) GT Labs. (0966010663). A fictionalized account of the great dinosaur fossil wars. Covers the efforts of Edward Drinker Cope and Othniel Charles Marsh and each of these scientist's efforts to find and collect the most fossils to make the most significant discoveries.

❑ Pekar, Harvey. **The Quitter**. (2005) DC Comics/Vertigo. (140120399X). An account of rising above a troubled youth and how one troubled youth saved himself from becoming a bully by writing.

❑ Powell, Eric. **Billy the Kid's Old-Timey Oddities**. (2006) Dark Horse Comics. (1593074484). Living a lonely existence after faking his own death, Billy the Kid is ripe for adventure. So when he has a "chance" meeting with an intermediary who wants him to protect a group of circus freaks as they go on a quest to steal an important jewel from Dr. Frankenstein himself.

❑ Quick, Jen Lee. **Off*Beat, Volume 1**. (2005) TOKYOPOP. (1598161326). Obsessed with his genius status and his need to learn about his new neighbor, Colin, Tory Blake's scheming leads him to some real mysteries. Who is Colin? Why is Colin so secretive? What does the Gaia Project have to do with Colin and what is the real relationship?

❑ Raiti, Ashly. **Mark of the Succubus Book 1**. (2005) TOKYOPOP. (1598162667). Living in the human world and attending high school to familiarize herself with the world in which she is expected to operate, Maeve finds herself in love with the guy who is her target. How will she succeed as a succubus-in-training if she cannot get around the rules of he demons which compel her?

❑ Rivkah, **Steady Beat, Volume 1**. (2005) TOKYOPOP. (1598161350). Leah's older sister is near perfect but then Leah finds a love letter addressed to her sister and signed "Love, Jessica." What does this mean? If her sister is gay, how will that affect her mother's career as a Republican State Texas Senator?

❑ Rollins, Prentis. **The Making of a Graphic Novel: The Resonator, Vol. 3.** (2006) Watson-Guptill Publications, Inc. (0823030539). In this science fiction world humans no longer need to sleep — it is a luxury and available only with drugs or the use of a resonator. When Bronson goes to a sleep center before a long mining expedition, he connects with a resonator who turns out to be a cat.

❑ Saki, Hiwatari. **Tower of the Future Volume 1**. (2005) DC Comics. (1401208142). A shocking deep family secret interrupts Takeru's goal of becoming a fantasy writer.

❑ Sfar, Joann. **Vampire Loves.** (2006) Roaring Book Press. (1596430931). Ferdinand, a vampire perhaps, has strange night behavior and strange relationships with his past and present girlfriends, all the while he is assisting police in solving a crime.

❑ Shakespeare, William. **Macbeth.** (2006) PenguinPuffin Graphics. (0142404098). A classic revisited and retold in graphic format.

❏ Siegel, Siena Cherson. *To Dance: A Ballerina's Graphic Novel*. (2006) Simon and Schuster, (1416926879). A timeline of a dancer's life—from the beginning to adult.

❏ Sizer, Paul. *Moped Army*. (2005) Café Digital. (0976856549). Set in 2277 when fuel is illegal, Simone is faced with leaving behind her pampered life and abusive relationship with her boyfriend and find a new life in the mile high city and siding with the moped army.

❏ Spears, Rick. *Dead West*. (2005) Gigantic Graphic Novels. (0976303817). A young Native American finds his tribe decimated by settlers, sets out for revenge, and attacks a small town with zombies.

❏ Stassen, J. P. *Deogratias: A Tale of Rwanda.* (2006) Roaring Brook Press First Second. (1596431032). Two teens, genocide, 1990s—a disturbing tale of chaos in Rwanda.

❏ Suenobu, Keiko. *Life: Volume One.* (2006) TOKYOPOP. (1595329315). It is her friend who should have made the cut. When Ayumu studies so she can make the prestigious high school to be with her friend, she makes the cut and her friend does not. Guilt and stress causes Ayumu to self-mutilate.

❏ Sumerak, Marc. *Ororo: Before the Storm Digest*. (2005) Marvel Enterprises. (0785118195). Ororo developed leadership skills as a member of the gang of child thieves in Cairo, but now she must use her skills to survive the mysterious Mr. Barrett's job offer.

❏ Takanashi, Mitsuba. *Crimson Hero.* (2005) VIZ Media/Shojo Beat Manga. (1421501406). Nobara's mother only wants her to be a traditional daughter and become a "young mistress" in the family restaurant. Nobara only cares about volleyball and actually transferred to Crimson Field High School. But her mother has some dirty tricks to play.

❏ Tomasi, Peter. *Light Brigade.* (2006) DC Comics. (1401207952). An elite band of WWII soldiers join with Centurion to retrieve the Sword of God from the zombie Nazis intent on using the Sword to destroy Heaven and Earth.

❏ Vaughan, Brian K. *Ex Machina Volume 2: Tag.* (2005) DC Comics/ Wildstorm Signature Series. (1401206263). More happenings with the superhero in his role as mayor of New York City. Explosions and disaster threaten the safety in the city.

❏ Vaughan, Brian K. *Runaways: Escape to New York Digest 5*. (2006) Marvel Enterprises. (0785119019). Includes issues #7–12. Cloak and Dagger are about to get some help from their friends "the Runaway Gang." Along the way the gang encounters Spider-man, Captain America, Iron Man, and Wolverine.

❏ Waid, Mark. *Legion of Super-Heroes: Teenage Revolution*. (2005) DC Comics. (1401204821). Set in the 31st Century, these teen-age heroes are poised to fight galactic tyranny.

❏ Waid, Mark. *Teen Titans, Volume 4: The Future Is Now*. (2005) DC Comics. (1401204759). Teen super-heroes find themselves fighting future versions of themselves.

❏ Watase, Yuu. *Absolute Boyfriend, Volume 1.* (2006) Viz Media. (1421500167). How will Riiko pay for the robot, the perfect new boyfriend? All she needed was one cute guy to ask her out, but now that the robot, Night, is here is it more problem than help?

❏ Weinstein, Lauren R. *Girl Stories.* (2006) Henry Holt and Company. (0805078630). Encounters with her first boyfriend, getting a piercing, and an examination of the age old question, "Am I fat?" comprise the basis for these short stories.

❑ Whitta, Gary. *Death, Jr.* (2005) Image Comics. (1582405263). The Grim Reaper's son wants nothing more than to make his Dad proud. Little does he know that a trip to the Supernatural Museum will unleash evil in the world.

❑ Wood, Brian. *Demo: The Collection.* (2005) AiT/Planet Lar. (1932051422). Twelve stories about young people with powers of possessing and abilities far greater than others. Decisions are the focus.

❑ Yang, Gene. *American Born Chinese.* (2006) Roaring Brook Press First Second. (1596431520). Jin Wang is Taiwanese and often sits alone in a corner of his schoolyard. Three seemingly unrelated tales share an unexpected connection to form a tale of self-acceptance and identity.

❑ Yazawa, AI. *Nana, Volume 2.* (2006) VIZ Media/ Shojo Beat Manga. (1421503786). Nana Komatsu and Nana Osaki are back in Tokyo in pursuit of their dreams to restart a music career and reconnect with friends.

❑ Yazawa, Ai. *Nana.* (2006) VIZ Media. (1421501082). Two teens meet in Tokyo—one is a punk rocker who is running from a broken heart and the other is a rather naïve blond who goes to Tokoyo to be with her boyfriend and to prove that she can make it on her own.

❑ Yoshinaga, Fumi. *Antique Bakery, Vol. 2.* (2005) Digital Manga Publishers. (1569709459). Hilarious and wacky—three co-workers (a pastry chef, the owner, and a sous-chef) engage in tomfoolery.

❑ Yoshinaga, Fumi. *Antique Bakery, Vol. 3.* (2006) Digital Manga Publishers. (1569709440). *Antique Bakery, Vol. 4.* Digital Manga Publishers. (1569709432). Two more volumes in the series of humor filled antics.

❑ You, Higuri. *Cantarella: Volume One. Go Comi!* (2005) Manga. (0976895706). Cesare Borgia is the mainstay of the Borgia Family and its evil reputation.

❑ You, Higuri. *Gorgeous Carat.* (2006) TOKYOPOP. (1598161024). Ray Balzac Courland forces Florian's mother to give him up. Who is Courland? And what does he want with Florian? Does Courland have any connection with the mysterious and dark thief Noir?

❑ Yumeka, Sumomo. *Same Cell Organism.* (2006) Digital Manga Publishers. (1569709262). Short stories, nicely illustrated. The first stories feature one pair and are especially interesting.

Section 4

Poetry & Verse Novels and Scripted Novels

Poetry & Verse Novels
Introduction

Poetry is for all places. In his *Pass the Poetry, Please* (Harper, 1987), Lee Bennett Hopkins says, "The unit approach is good for social studies, science, and mathematics, but not for poetry." Hopkins and other poets implore educators not to reduce poetry to an assignment, not to reduce the poetry unit to a sequence introducing a structure or form and then asking students to "write a haiku" or whatever form is being studied. The substance of good poetry is not its form but rather what is said (and not said). Surround young readers and listeners with all forms of poetry, giving them the rhythm and language of the form while allowing their own writing to take whatever form is most appropriate.

In April of each year the Academy of American Poets sponsors National Poetry Month. In concert with the Academy of American Poets, the Center for the Book in the Library of Congress designates the third week of April as Young People's Poetry Week.

For more information about National Poetry Month and Young People's Poetry Week go to the Academy of American Poets website (http://www.poets.org) and The Children's Book Council (http://www.cbcbooks.org).

In the past few years an interesting trend in young adult literature has developed: novels written in blank verse have made inroads in attracting readers. A huge number of these books address dealing with contemporary social issues, letting readers see the problems in a new light, and encouraging readers to reveal their own emotions in a similar poetic form.

Credited with starting this lasting trend are some very popular novels from the past few years:

Love That Dog by Sharon Creech (Joanna Cotler, 2001)
Out of the Dust by Karen Hesse (Scholatic, 1997)
Locomotion by Jacqueline Woodsong (Putnam, 2003)
Carver: A Life in Poems by Marilyn Nelson (Hand Print, 2001)
Fortune's Bones: The Manumission Requiem by Marilyn Nelson (Hand Print, 2004)

The following list includes both collections/anthologies of poems and narratives written in blank verse.

Poetry and Verse Novels—Update 2007

Gary Soto—Poet Pick for 2007

Soto, Gary. (2006) *A Fire in My Hands*. Harcourt. (0152055649). Originally published in 1971 and unavailable since 1998, this reissued volume now contains a short interview with the poet that is appended at the end. Sixteen poems are new to the collection, and 16 poems from the original edition are reworked and expanded.

Carlson, Lori. (2005) *Red Hot Salsa: Bilingual Poems in Being Young and Latino in The United States*. Henry Holt. (0805076166)
Shortly after the tenth anniversary of the publication of *Cool Salsa* (Holt, 1994), this companion title was released. Carlson includes established poets such as **Gary Soto**, Martin Espada, and Luis J. Rodriguez, some new voices, and a few poems by students in the New York Public School system.

❏ Adoff, Jaime. *Jimi and Me*. (2005) Hyperion/Jump at the Sun. (0786852143). 336 pgs. Keith and his father, a record producer, had shared their mutual admiration of Jimi Hendrix and their love of his music. In the six months since his father's tragic (and violent) death, Keith has dealt with his grief, his mother's decision to move to Ohio to live with his aunt, and a racist bully in the small town where they have retreated. Keith discovers that his father had a second family with another son—a son named Jimi. Keith feels betrayed but the episode at Cleveland's Rock & Roll Hall of Fame is effective.

❏ Carvell, Marlene. *Sweetgrass Basket*. (2005) Dutton. (0525475478). 256 pgs. At the turn of the twentieth century Mattie and Sarah's father send his children off to the Carlisle Indian Boarding School in Pennsylvania. Mattie is falsely accused of stealing and is beaten and shamed. Always admonished to become more like "white people," Mattie and Sarah tell their stories in alternating voices. Based on the author's husband's Mohawk family experiences at Carlisle.

❏ Connor, Leslie. *Dead on Town Line*. (2005) Illustrated by Gina Triplett. Dial. (0803730217) 131 pgs. A teen murder victim narrates her story from her afterlife. When Cassie is murdered she is left hidden in a crevice. She encounters the ghost of Birdie, another murdered girl who was hidden in the same crevice years earlier. Together the girls are able to help Cassie's family and friends reach closure and finish Cassie's piano composition—something she had left unfinished.

❏ Frost, Helen. *The Braid*. (2006) Farrar, Straus & Giroux/Frances Foster Books. (0374309620) 112 pgs. The poetic voices of two sisters are intertwined (braided) together just as their hair was braided as a symbol of their connection. Despite the fact that when their family is evicted from the Western Isles of Scotland (1850), Jeannie goes with her siblings and parents to Canada and Sarah stays behind with Grandma. Tragic events on the ocean crossing and life in a new land echo against the hardships endured in Scotland. Home, shelter, and heritage all braided together, though oceans apart. A stirring metaphor played out in rhyme and rhythm.

❑ Grimes, Nikki. *Dark Sons.* (2005) Hyperion/Jump at the Sun. (0786818883). 224 pgs. Sam, an African-American teen, must find a way to deal with his parents' divorce and his relationship with his father (and new white step-mother; and the baby half-brother named Sam). This plot mimics the theme of the biblical story of Ishmael, son of Abraham, and his despair upon being replaced by Isaac.

❑ Herrera, Juan Felipe. *Downtown Boy.* (2005) Scholastic. (0439644895) 304 pgs. Lines of verse to poems create a lyrical tale that recounts the year of Juanito Palomares in the late-1950s in California. Juanito's father is a roving man and that means Juanito and his mother first live in San Francisco with relatives, then in San Diego in many different homes.

❑ Janeczko, Paul B. *A Kick in the Head: An Everyday Guide to Poetic Forms.* (2005) Illustrated by Chris Raschka. Candlewick. (0763606626) 64 pgs. Clear and very concise explanations of many poetic forms. Each form is defined, an example presented, and an illustration.

❑ Janeczko, Paul B. and J. Patrick Lewis. *Wing Nuts: Screwy Haiku.* (2006) Illustrated by Tricia Tusa. Little, Brown. (0316607312) 32 pgs. This collection of Japanese verse form, senryu, is similar to the haiku form, except that this form tends to be people-oriented rather than nature focuses. Funny, witty, and often takes a somewhat sophisticated reader to understand the wordplay.

❑ Marsalis, Wynton. *Jazz A-B-Z: An A to Z Collection of Jazz Portraits*. (2005) Illustrated by Paul Rogers. Candlewick. (0763621358). 76 pgs. Twenty-six Jazz greats are included in alliterative poetry. Rogers' large illustrations illuminate the poems.

❑ Myers, Walter Dean. *Street Love*. (2006) Armistad. (0060280808). 144 pgs. When their mother is sentenced to 25 years in prison, Junice and her younger sister know that foster care is not far way. Uncertain as to their future, Junice is not sure about how to react to the arrival of Damien, a student-athlete whose future has already been decided by his mother. Junice has an unclear future and Damien has a planned future. What kind of a relationship can they have? And what of the future? A compelling verse novel from a highly successful YA author.

❑ Smith, Kirsten. *The Geography of Girlhood.* (2006) Little, Brown, 2006. (0316160210). 192 pgs. Penny's mother abandoned her when she was just six. Now in high school, Penny still longs for her mother but also has to deal with adolescence: a depressed friend, her first boyfriend's accidental death, an older and wild sister, and a new step-mother. It seems like everything in her life is a mistake, including her decision to runaway with her sister's ex-boyfriend. Coming home she finds that there is more to life than what she has seen so far. A verse novel.

❑ Stone, Tanya Lee. *A Bad Boy Can be Good for a Girl*. (2006) Random House/Wendy Lamb. (0385747020). 240 pgs. A popular jock manages to seduce and then drop Josie, a freshman who normally values her girlfriends over boys; Nicolette, who views her own sexuality as a point of power; and finally Aviva, a pretty, smart, and artsy senior. When he summarily dumps each of them they begin to realize what love and sex is all about. A few blank pages at the end of the book holds handwritten notes that reveal each of their thoughts. Sex scenes (although not graphic) may make this more appropriate for mature readers—but given a chance it will be passed from teenage girl to teenage girl. Free verse.

Scripted Novels
Introduction

Scripted novels have made their entrance close on the heels of the popularity of the verse novel. A scripted novel is one that includes some aspects of the drama form: screenwriting, playwriting, monologue, or even poetry. Teen readers have often been asked to familiarize themselves with plays and drama form. Units of study feature Shakespeare's plays (particulary *Midsummer Night's Dream* and *Romeo and Juliet*) and other more recent classics as in *Inherit the Wind*, *A Raisin in the Sun*, and *The Miracle Worker*, to name a few. In recent years the drama offerings have become more accessible to today's readers. In the few years immediately preceding 2007, there were several scripted novels published. The trend might have begun with Avi's 1991 novel *Nothing But the Truth* (Scholastic) and his 1992 novel *Who Was That Masked Man Anyway* (Scholastic). That full-length novel was for an intermediate audience, but its immense popularity stimulated a style that many other authors began to experiment with. Scripted novels take various forms. The book might include large chunks of a play script or may be written entirely as a performance script, and several variations in-between.

Touchstones in the area of scripted novels include books by Paul Fleischman—a master with the form:

Joyful Noise: Poems for Two Voices (HarperCollins, 1988)—Reader's Theater Piece

Bull Run. (HarperCollins, 1993)—Reader's Theater Piece

Seedfolks. (HarperCollins, 1997)—Reader's Theater Piece

Mind's Eye. (Holt, 1999)—script novel

Seek. (Cricket, 2001)—script novel

Breakout. (Cricket, 2004)—performance art novel

Walter Dean Myers's also experiemented with the reader's theater form early on when he wrote **Monster** (HarperCollins, 1999) and **Here in Harlem** (Holiday House, 2004).

Now that scripted novels have gained recognition there seems to be a natural transition to the graphic novel many professionals were avoiding as too juvenile. For recent lists of graphic novels see Section 3.

A Sampling of recent titles that play with the new fenre of Scripted Novels follows.

❑ Almond, David. *Two Plays*. (2005) Delacorte. (0385730748) 240 pgs. Within the pages of this book is a dramatization of Almond's prose novel *Skellig* (Delacorte, 1999) as well as a dramatization of *Wild Girl, Wild Boy*. In the latter play, Elaine has lost her father and attempts to deal with her grief by forming an alliance with "the wild boy." Giving way to fantasy, the two build a new life. *Skellig* also deals with fantasy when he retreats to the old dilapidated garage and meets Skellig here. An author's note appended at the end of the book provides information about the subtleties of writing drama as opposed to writing prose.

❑ Creech, Sharon. *Replay*. (2005) Joanna Cotler. (006050192) 240 pgs. A section at the end of *Replay* includes the entire play, thus presenting a subtle invitation for producing the play in the classroom. Leonardo's family calls him "Sardine" – the twelve-year-old is packed between his siblings. Then a mystery unfolds: who is that woman in his father's family picture? Leonardo is also preparing for the school's play and his own chaotic home life seems to have some parallels.

❑ Fleischman, Paul. *Zap: A Play*. (2005) Candlewick. (0763627747) 96 pgs. This is a book written for the stage. A real spoof on all the conventions of stage. Mix in a little Shakespeare with a touch of Chekhov, Tennessee Williams, Agatha Christie, and Neil Simon. The characters cavort through the scenes, in and out, and end up merging into one chaotic meleé.

❑ Koja, Kathe. *Talk*. (2005) Farrar, Straus and Giroux. (0374373825). 144 pgs. Kit Webster is in the closet and desperately needs a break. He decides to escape his reality by seeking a lead in the school play.

Drama queen Lindsay Walsh plays opposite Kit and between their alternating voices readers come to understand the chemistry between each of their roles. In points the dialogue seems didactic but will raise a stream of consciousness.

❑ Lester, Julius. *Day of Tears*. (2005) Hyperion/Jump At the Sun. (0786804904) 92 pgs. A novel that includes a "dialogue"—more aligned with a reader's theater script. This book is a touchstone for this genre, blending monologues and scenes. The day comes in 1859 when Pierce Butler puts his "chattel" on the auction block. The monologues swirl around Emma, one of the slaves sold that day. The characterization is strong and believable. Readers will care about Emma's future and the future of others met within the pages of the book.

❑ Mazer, Norma Fox. *What I Believe*. (2005) Harcourt. (0152014624). 176 pgs. A form somewhat different than the others in this list; this novel is a collage of poems, journal entries, letters, lists, monologues, and dialogues. While not scripted in the general sense, this novel's varied form lends itself to performance. Vicki's father absents himself from his family and Vicki is forced to survive in a new neighborhood and new school. Trying to be normal is hard to do.

❑ Park, Linda Sue. *Project Mulberry*. (2005) Clarion. A large portion of this narrative includes scripted conversations between the author and the chief protagonist. As Julia Song and her friend Patrick move through their school activity involving raising silk works, Julia has side conversations with the author who discusses the ins and outs of writing the story itself. What decisions does the author have to make? What is the genesis of the ideas that evolve throughout?

Section 5

Illustrated Short Stories (Picture Books for Teens)

Illustrated Short Stories
Introduction

The texts of picture books are very similar to the short stories found within anthologies of stories collected and packaged for older readers. The only difference between the short story texts and the texts of those found in picture books are the illustrations.

Novels often have several conflicts within one tale while short stories or picture books generally have room for just one. Collections of short stories are wonderful for emphasizing a particular theme or curricular connection. Even though a picture book contains one story, the possibilities for connections are the same. Short stories (illustrated or not) can be used to:

- promote literacy across the curriculum;
- convey ideas simply;
- encourage the reading of more difficult books on the same subject;
- encourage creative writing in prose and poetry;
- promote awareness of language;
- teach artistic styles in illustrations;
- encourage the development of creativity and imagination;
- introduce a person or topic for more in-depth study;
- provide a schema for students in special education or ESL classes;
- provide models for teen parents to read to their children;
- teach elements of literature: plotting, characterization;
- provide material for reader's theater, speech class, and so forth;
- teach literary devices: foreshadowing, flashbacks, and so forth.

In order to became more familiar with this genre and potentials for use, you may wish to seek out some of the following resources which will provide additional rationale and provide lists of picture books that are important additions to the lists that follow.

- Carr, Kathryn S., et. al. "Not Just for the Primary Grades: A Bibliography of Picture Books for Secondary Content Teachers." *Journal of Adolescent & Adult Literacy*, 10813004, Oct2001, Vol. 45, Issue 2.
- Giorgis, Cyndi. "The Power of Reading Picture Books Aloud to Secondary Students." *Clearing House*, 00098655, Sep/Oct99, Vol. 73, Issue 1.
- Henry, Robin and Carol Simpson. "Picture Books & Older Readers: A Match Made in Heaven." *Teacher Librarian.* 28:3 (Feb 2001): 23-38.
- Johnson, Keith. "Children's Books in a High School Library? A Risky Question Worth Asking." *The Book Report* 19.5 (2001): 6–8. (Includes a great list of picture books from past years).
- Matthews, Rene. "What Picture Books Do You Recommend for Use in the English Language Arts Classroom." *English Journal* 88.4 (1999): 27–33.
- Neal, Judith C., and Kay Moore. "The Very Hungry Caterpillar meets Beowulf in the secondary classroom." *Journal of Reading* 35 (1992): 290–296.
- Osborn, Sunya "Picture Books for Young Adult Readers." *The ALAN Review* 28: 3, (2001) p. 24.

On the Web
- Coiro, Julie. "Using Picture Books with Middle and High School Students. " Suite 101.com. (Online) Accessed September 6, 2006 http://www.suite101.com/article.cfm/readng/47355/6

In the list that follows, I've picked a few of my favorite titles for 2007, published in the last few years—titles that will invariably present some ideas to you for making curriculum connections. The articles cited above will have many archival suggestions from past publishing years.

Picture Books That Have Possibilities for Integration
A Few of My Favorites for 2007

> "One of the great things about books is sometimes there are some fantastic pictures."
> — George W. Bush (43rd USA President)

❑ Bardoe, Cheryl. *Gregor Mendel: The Friar Who Grew Peas*. (2006) Illustrated by Joseph A. Smith. Abrams. (08100954753) 40 pgs. A look at the life of the man who is known as the Father of Modern Genetics. A great introduction to hereditary factors with gloriously accurate illustrations that clearly illuminate the basic pattern of hereditary. Pair with the book length account of the same topic: *The Monk in the Garden: The Lost and Found Genius of Gregor Mendel* by Robin Marantz Henig. (Houghton Mifflin, 2000; 224 pgs; 0395977657)

❑ Collard, Sneed B. *The Prairie Builders: Reconstructing America's Lost Grasslands*. (2005) Photographs by Sneed B. Collard. Houghton. (061839687X). 72 pgs. Follows the work at the Neal Smith National Wildlife Refuge (Iowa) and the efforts to restore the prairie. Covers the successes and the failures. The book documents efforts over a number of years.

❑ Gibbons, Gail. *Ice Cream: The Full Scoop*. (2006) Holiday House. (13: 9780823420001) 32 pgs. From it's origins and the involvement of Marco Polo, to it's evolution as iced cream, Gail Gibbons follows the "The Ice Cream Business," from milking the cows to a tour of an ice cream factory to the grocery store. Use this as a model for creating sequential explanation of how other everyday foods items are created/manufactured.

❑ Janeczko, Paul B., ed. *A Kick in the Head: An Everyday Guide to Poetic Forms*. (2005) Illustrated by Chris Raschka. Candlewick. (0763606626). 64 pgs. Defines and illustrates poetic forms and gives a classic example of each form. Use as a model for one's own search for an example and an art poster activity, or for writing,

❑ McCully, Emily Arnold. *Marvelous Mattie: How Margaret E. Knight Became an Inventor.* (2006) Farrar Straus Giroux. (0374348103). 32 pgs. Sketch books, prototypes, and the patent process are all detailed in this book about a female inventor who began as a young girl by inventing a shuttle cock shut-off that saved many lives to inventing a way of folding a paper bag so as to make it sit flat for use. Pairs nicely with *Margaret Knight, Girl Inventor* by Marlene Targ Brill (Millbrook Press, 2001; 32 pgs. 07613117562)

❑ McCutcheon, John. *Christmas in the Trenches*. (2006) Illustrated by Henri Sorensen. Peachtree. (1561453749). 32 pgs. with CD. Fictionalized account of the Christmas truce that occurred during World War I in 1914. Establishes a discussion point for the events that occur during years of war.

❑ Silverstein, Shel. *Runny Babbit: A Billy Sook*. (2005) HarperCollins. (0060256532). CD 70 minutes. (2006) Read by Dennis Locorriere. HarperCollins. (0060823968). Published after Silverstein's death, this book was completed prior to his death in 1999 and is populated by some interesting characters: populated by the likes of Runny Babbit, Toe Jurtle, Ploppy Sig, Polly Dorkupine, and Pilly Belican (who owns the Sharber Bop). Silverstein worked on this "billy sook" for over 20 years. A sophisticated look at language and the aspect of consonant substitution.

❑ Smith, Lane. *John, Paul, George, & Ben*. (2006) Hyperion Books for Children. (0786848936) 32 pgs. Readers will have to know something about the history of these four lads: John [Hancock], Paul [Revere], George [Washington], and Ben [Franklin] (and about Thomas Jefferson who was always off doing his own thing) in order to understand the satire and play on the events that occurred (or didn't occur). Allusion to the British four lads (The Beatles) and their recording of Abbey.

❑ Taylor, Gaylia. *George Crum and the Saratoga Chip.* (2006) Illustrated by Frank Morrison. Lee & Low. (1584302550). 32 pgs. A fictionalized account of the invention of potato chips by George Crum, an African-America/Native American chef. Pairs nicely with: Stowell, Penelope. (2005) *The Greatest Potatoes.* Illustrated by Sharon Watts. Jump at the Sun. (0786851139} 36 pgs. www.ideafinder.com/history/inventions/potatochips.htm.

❑ Truss, Lynne. *Eats, Shoots & Leaves: Why, Commas Really Do Make a Difference.* (2006) Illustrated by Bonnie Timmons. Putnam. (03992244913). Truss uses identical sentences sans commas and shows how a missing or misplaced comma can create very different meanings. Timmons's illustrations illuminate the humorous effects of the errant commas. Try using this book to help illustrate the six-traits of writing. Picture book version of Truss's adult book *Eats, Shoots & Leaves: The Zero Tolerance Approach to Punctuation* (Gotham, 2004).

❑ Weatherford, Carole Boston. *A Negro League Scrapbook.* (2005) Boyds Mills Press. (1590780914). 48 pgs. Poetic tributes to the Negro Leagues are augmented with statistics, anecdotes, player profiles, and historic images. Inspired by the author's trip to the Negro League Baseball Museum in Kansas City, Missouri. An important book for introducing the topic of civil rights, Negro Baseball Leagues, baseball, prejudice, Jim Crow era, and a number of other related topics.

❑ Winter, Jeanette. *Mama: A True Story, in which a Baby Hippo Loses his Mama During a Tsunami, but Finds a New Home, and a New Mama.* (2006) Harcourt. (0152054952) Hatkoff, Isabelle and Craid Hatkoff. *Owen and Mzee: The True Story of a Remarkable Friendship*. (2006) Scholastic. (0439829739). Morris, Ann. (2005) *Tsunami.* Photography by Heidi Larson. Lerner. (0761395016). This package of three books deal with the tsunami in Indonesia and off the coast of Kenya. The Owen and Mzee story is a true story of animals and their care for one another, while the Morris account is the story of two boys who forge a friendship while dealing with the aftermath of the Tsunami. Great discussion and research starter.

Section 6

Audio Material for Teens

Audio Material for Teens
Introduction

Using audio readings of books have enabled teachers to build a community of readers and participate in initiatives similar to the one book/one class project, general classroom reads, and so forth. Encouraging and making possible the ability of less-able readers to use an audio book to read a book-length novel that other students are also reading encourages group interaction and heterogeneous group discussions. Audio books, whether on tape or audio CD, allow learning disabled students to read more and to read at their age and interest level. Audio books are able to reduce frustration and fatigue often experienced by readers who are struggling with vocabulary and comprehension. Although we recommend that audio books be used in conjunction with independent reading (with the requirement that students follow along in the text as much as possible), there seems no question that audio books provide another voice, keeping reluctant readers interested and helping them move at an even pace throughout the narrative. The assistance of audio books often encourages less-able readers to read a longer book than they would read by themselves.

Using audio books:

- Provides modeling of fluent reading for students who have fluency issues.

- Allows less able readers to enjoy a selection and participate in appropriate discussions with his or her peers.

- Allows a marginal reader to become acquainted with the book and its content before being asked to participate in classroom activities, i.e. reading and discussing the book in the classroom.

- Allows various levels of readers and allows readers to "read" the book while traveling, exercising, or engaging in alternative activities.

- Provides an alternative method of presentation to accommodate alternative learning styles.

- Varies the classroom presentation.

- Minimizes the struggle for students with disabilities.

- Assists in vocabulary building.

Additional resources:

Allen, Janet. *Yellow Brick Roads: Shared and Guided Paths to Independent Reading 4-12.* Stenhouse Publishers, 2000. pgs. 108–109.

Allen, Janet and Kyle Gonzalez. *There's Room for Me Here: Literacy Workshop in the Middle School.* Stenhouse Publishers, 1998. pgs. 31–32.

Lamb, Annette and Larry Johnson (2002; updated 2005) "Multimedia Seeds: Exploring Audio and Video Collections—Audio Books." Adapted from Lamb, A. (2002). Building Treehouses for Learning. Vision to Action. (Online) http://eduscapes.com/seeds/audiobooks.html

Audio Books in the Classroom/Library

❑ Abrahams, Peter. **Down the Rabbit Hole: An Echo Falls Mystery**. Read by Mandy Siegfried, trade edition: HarperChildren's Audio, 2005. 8 hours. (7 discs, 0060786647) or library edition: Recorded Books, 2005. (7 discs, 141936815X, 6 cassettes, 14193576).

❑ Anderson, Laurie Halse. **Prom**. Read by Katherine Kellgren. Recorded Books, 2005. 5.75 hours. (5 discs, 1419356100, 4 cassettes, 1419350978).

❑ Avi. **Poppy's Return**. Read by John McDonough. Recorded Books, 2006. 4.5 hours. (3 cassettes, 1419371185).

❑ Bajoria, Paul. **The Printer's Devil**. Read by Katherine Kellgren. Recorded Books, 2005. 9.25 hours. (8 discs, 1419366238; 7 cassettes, 1419366181).

❑ Banks, Lynne Reid. **Tiger, Tiger**. Read by Jan Francis. Listening Library, 2005. 5 hours, 3 minutes. (4 discs, 0307246380, 3 cassettes, 0307245462).

❑ Bauer, Joan. **Best Foot Forward**. Read by Kathe Mazur. Listening Library, 2005. 4 hours, 35 minutes. (4 discs, 0307246299; 3 cassettes, 0307246124).

❑ Beard, Philip. **Dear Zoe, A Novel**. Read by Cassandra Morris. HighBridge, 2005. 4 hours, 45 minutes. (5 discs, 1565119428).

❑ Bodett, Tom. **Norman Tuttle on the Last Frontier: A Novel in Stories**. Read by Tom Bodett. Listening Library, 2004. 4 hours, 40 minutes. (4 discs, 140009495X, 3 cassettes 1400090571).

❑ Cabot, Meg. **Princess in Training**. Read by Clea Lewis. Listening Library, 2005. 6 hours, 17 minutes. (6 discs, 030720670X, 4 cassettes, 1400098769).

❑ Cabot, Meg. **Ready or Not**. Read by Ariadne Meyers. Listening Library, 2005. 6 hours, 27 minutes. (6 discs, 0307246140; 4 cassettes, 0307243370).

❑ Cameron, Ann. **Colibrí**. Read by Jacqueline Kim. Listening Library, 2004. 4 hours, 45 minutes. (3 cassettes, 1400085365, 5 discs, 140008993X).

❑ Card, Orson Scott. **Shadow of the Giant**. Read by David Birney, Scott Brick, and cast. Audio Renaissance, 2005. 12 hours. (10 discs, 1593974965).

❑ Colfer, Eoin. **Artemis Fowl: The Opal Deception**. Read by Nathaniel Parker. Listening Library, 2005. 7.5 hours. (6 discs, 0307243338, 5 cassettes, 0307243311).

❑ Delaney, Joseph. **The Last Apprentice: Revenge of the Witch**. Read by Christopher Evan Welch. Trade edition: HarperChildren's Audio, 2006. 5.25 hours. (5 discs, 0060824026); library edition: Recorded Books, 2006. (5 discs, 1419384465; 5 cassettes, 1419384414).

❑ Dessen, Sara. **Truth About Forever**. Read by Stina Nielsen. Recorded Books, 2005. 12 hours, 30 minutes. (8 discs, 141933879X, 9 cassettes, 1419326481).

❑ Dessen, Sarah. **Just Listen**. Read by Jennifer Ikeda. Recorded Books, 2006. 12 hours. (11 discs. 1419394401; 9 cassettes. 1419394355).

❑ Dhami, Narinder. **Bindi Babes**. Read by Nina Wadia. Listening Library, 2004. 4 hours, 21 minutes. (4 cassettes, 1400085381).

❑ Farmer, Nancy. **The Sea of Trolls**. Read by Gerard Doyle. Recorded Books, 2004. 14 hours. (12 discs, 1419308203, 10 cassettes, 1419320904).

❑ Flanagan, John. *The Ruins of Gorlan: The Ranger's Apprentice, Book One.* Read by John Keating. Recorded Books, 2006. 7.75 hours. (7 discs, 1419393995; 6 cassettes, 1419393944.

❑ Friend, Natasha. *Perfect.* Read by Danielle Ferland. Recorded Books, 2005. 4.5 hours. (4 discs, 1419370189; 3 cassettes, 1419370138).

❑ Funke, Cornelia. *Inkspell.* Read by Brendan Fraser. Listening Library, 2005. 18 hours, 46 minutes. (16 discs, 0307282929; 11 cassettes, 0307282910).

❑ Gaiman, Neil. *Anansi Boys.* Read by Lenny Henry. HarperAudio, 2005. 10 hours. (8 discs, 0060823844).

❑ Gardne, Graham. *Inventing Elliot.* Read by Dominic Taylor, Listening Library, 2004. 4 hours, 45 minutes. (4 cassettes, 1807223204).

❑ Giff, Patricia Reilly. *Willow Run.* Read by Staci Snell. Listening Library, 2005. 3 hours, 20 minutes. (3 discs, 030728333X; 2 cassettes, 0307282996).

❑ Grant, K.M. *Blood Red Horse: Book 1 of the deGranville Trilogy.* Read by Maggie Mash. Recorded Books, 2005. 9.75 hours. (9 discs, 1419356062, 7 cassettes, 141935115X).

❑ Grant, K.M. *Green Jasper: Book 2 of the deGranville Trilogy.* Read by Maggie Mash, Recorded Books, 2006. 8 hours. (8 discs, 1419394703; 6 cassettes, 1419394657).

❑ Gruber, Michael. *The Witch's Boy.* Read by Denis O'Hare. HarperChildren's Audio, 2005. 8 hours. (7 discs, 0060785969).

❑ Hale, Marian. *The Truth About Sparrows.* Read by Emily Janice Card. Listening Library, 2005. 5 hours, 36 minutes. (4 cassettes, 030720720X).

❑ Han, Jenny. *Shug.* Read by Liz Morton. Recorded Books, 2006. 6 hours. (5 discs, 1419382489; 4 cassettes, 1419382438).

❑ Hautman, Pete. *Invisible.* Read by Norm Lee. Recorded Books, 2006. 3.75 hours. (3 discs, 1419384562; 3 cassettes, 1419384511).

❑ Hearn, Julie. *The Minister's Daughter.* Read by Heather O'Neill. Listening Library, 2005. 8 hours, 20 minutes. (7 discs, 0307246256, 5 cassettes, 0307245993).

❑ Hiaasen, Carl. *Flush.* Read by Michael Welch. Listening Library, 2005. 5 hours, 23 minutes. (5 discs, 0307282902, 4 cassettes, 0307282899).

❑ Horowitz, Anthony. *Ark Angel.* Read by Simon Prebble, Recorded Books, 2006. 8 hours. (7 discs, 1419394304; 6 cassettes, 1419394258).

❑ Horowitz, Anthony. *Raven's Gate: Book One of the Gatekeepers.* Read by Simon Prebble, Recorded Books, 2005. 7.25 hours. (6 discs, 1419355538, 5 cassettes, 1419350498).

❑ Horvath, Polly. *The Vacation.* Read by Kirby Heyborne. Listening Library, 2005. 4 hours, 43 minutes. (4 discs, 0307283623; 3 cassettes, 0307283615).

❑ Ihimaera, Witi. *Whale Rider.* Read by Jay Laga'aia. Bolinda Audio, 2005. 3 hours, 40 minutes. (4 discs, 1740935586).

❑ Johnson, Angela. *Bird.* Read by Chantale Hosein, Kamahl Palmer, and Matthew Pavich, Listening Library, 2004. 2 hours, 10 minutes. (2 discs, 1400099269, 2 cassettes, 1400099250).

❑ Koja, Kathe. *Buddha Boy.* Read by Spencer Murphy and the Full Cast Family. Full Cast Audio, 2004. 2 hours, 45 minutes. (3 discs, 1932076530).

❑ Korman, Gordon. *Born to Rock*. Read by Billy Hammond. Brilliance Audio, 2006. 5 hours. (5 discs, 1423311965, 4 cassettes, 1423311949).

❑ Lawrence, Iain. *B for Buster*. Read by Jeff Woodman. Recorded Books, 2005. 8.5 hours. (8 discs, 1419387669, 6 cassettes, 1419354744).

❑ Lawrence, Iain. *The Cannibals*. Read by John Keating. Recorded Books, 2006. 6.75 hours. (5 cassettes, 1419371584).

❑ Lawrence, Iain. *The Convicts*. Read by John Keating. Recorded Books, 2005. 6.75 hours. (6 discs, 1419367145; 5 cassettes, 1419367099).

❑ Limb, Sue. *Girl, (Nearly) 16: Absolute Torture*. Read by Katherine Kellgren. Listening Library, 2005. 5.75 hours. (5 discs, 0307246264, 4 cassettes, 0307207099).

❑ Lupica, Mike. *Travel Team*. Read by Oliver Wyman. Listening Library, 2005. 7 hours, 6 minutes. (6 discs, 0307283771, 4 cassettes, 0307283763).

❑ MacHale, D.J. *Pendragon, Book 1, The Merchant of Death*. Read by William Dufris, Brilliance, 2005. 12 hours. (10 discs, 1597372382).

❑ Mack, Tracy. *Birdland.* Read by Dion Graham. Blackstone Audiobooks, 2005. 3 hours. (3 discs, 0786176806, 3 cassettes, 0786136936).

❑ Marsden, John. *So Much to Tell You*. Read by Kate Hosking. Bolinda Audio, 2005. 3 hours, 25 minutes. (3 discs, 1740937198).

❑ Matthews, L.S. *Fish*. Read by J. Lamia. Listening Library, 2004. 3 hours, 13 minutes. (3 discs, 1400089883, 2 cassettes, 1400085217).

❑ McAllister, M.I. *Urchin of the Riding Stars: The Mistmantle Chronicles, Book One*. Read by Andrew Sachs. Listening Library, 2006. 7.5 hours. (6 discs, 0307206777, 4 cassettes, 1400098971).

❑ McCaughrean, Geraldine. *Stop the Train!* Read by Ellen Myrick and the Full Cast Family. Full Cast Audio, 2005. 7 hours, 50 minutes. (8 discs, 1933322438).

❑ McNamee, Graham. *Acceleration*. Read by Scott Brick. Listening Library, 2005. 5.5 hours. (5 discs, 0307207331, 4 cassettes, 0307207323).

❑ Meyer, Stephanie. *Twilight*. Read by Ilyana Kadushin. Listening Library, 2005. 13 hours. (11 discs, 0307282961, 8 cassettes, 0307282953).

❑ Mitchell, Elyne. *Silver Brumby's Daughter*. Read by Caroline Lee. Bolinda Audio, 2005. 7 hours, 55 minutes. (6 discs, 1740936884).

❑ Mlynowski, Sarah. *Bras & Broomsticks*. Read by Arlene Meyers, Listening Library, 2005. 8 hours, 11 minutes. (7 discs, 030720684X, 6 cassettes, 1400098793).

❑ Myers, Walter Dean. *Autobiography of My Dead Brother*. Read by J.D. Jackson. Recorded Books, 2006. 4.25 hours. (4 discs, 1419384767, 3 cassettes, 1419384716).

❑ O'Roark, Frances Dowell. *Chicken Boy*. Read by Stephen Hoye. Listening Library, 2005. 3 hours, 52 minutes. (4 disks, 0307246205, 3 cassettes, 0307246191).

❑ Patterson, James. *Maximum Ride: The Angel Experiment*. Read by Nancy Wu and Ed Sala. Recorded Books, 2005. 9.75 hours. (8 discs, 1419338447, 7 cassettes, 1419336290).

❑ Paver, Michelle. **Wolf Brother: Chronicles of Ancient Darkness, Book One**. Read by Ian McKellan. Trade edition, HarperChildren's Audio, 2005. 6.5 hours. (6 discs, 0060758384); library edition, Recorded Books, 2005; (6 discs, 1419338080, 5 cassettes, 1419326260).

❑ Peck, Richard. **Here Lies the Librarian.** Read by Lara Everly. Random House Audio Publishing Group, 2006. Unabridged. 4 hours, 30 minutes. (4 disks, 0307284069)

❑ Peck, Richard. **The Teacher's Funeral: A Comedy in Three Parts**. Read by Dylan Baker. Listening Library, 2004. 4 hours, 42 minutes. (5 discs, 1400094968, 4 cassettes, 1400091039).

❑ Perkins, Lynn Rae. **Criss Cross.** Read by Danielle Ferland. trade edition: HarperChildren's Audio, 2006. 9.5 hours. (6 discs, 0061161195) or library edition: Recorded Books 2006. (6 discs, 141939911X, 7 cassettes, 1419399063).

❑ Philbrick, Rodman. **The Young Man and the Sea**. Read by Kirby Heyborne. Listening Library, 2004. 3 hours, 48 minutes. (3 cassettes, 140094607).

❑ Reinhardt, Dana. **A Brief Chapter in My Impossible Life**. Read by Mandy Siegfried. Listening Library, 2006. 5.5 hours. (5 discs, 0307285669, 4 cassettes, 0307285650).

❑ Sachar, Louis. **Small Steps**. Read by Curtis McClarin. Listening Library, 2006. 6.25 hours. (5 discs, 0307282262, 3 cassettes, 0307282252).

❑ Schmidt, Gary D. **Lizzie Bright and the Buckminster Boy**. Read by Sam Freed. Listening Library, 2005. 6 hours, 49 minutes. (6 discs, 0307281833).

❑ Schmidt, Gary. **First Boy**. Read by Jesse Berns. Listening Library, 2005. 4.47 hours. (4 discs, 030728437, 3 cassettes, 0307283429).

❑ Stroud, Jonathan. **Ptolemy's Gate: The Bartimaeus Trilogy, Book Three**. Read by Simon Jones. Listening Library, 2006. 15 hours, 33 minutes. (13 discs, 0307285723, 10 cassettes, 0307285715).

❑ Trueman, Terry. **Cruise Control**. Read by Andy Paris, Recorded Books, 2005. 3.5 hours. (3 cassettes, 1419331094).

❑ Verne, Jules. **Around the World in 80 Days.** Read by Jim Dale. Listening Library, 2004. 7 hours, 53 minutes. (7 discs, 0307206823, 5 cassettes, 0307206289)

❑ Wooding, Chris. **Poison**. Read by Virginia Leishman. Recorded Books, 2006. 9.5 hours. (8 discs, 141939911X, 7 cassettes, 1419399063).

❑ Zevin, Gabrielle. **Elsewhere**. Read by Cassandra Morris. Listening Library, 2005. 7 hours, 3 minutes. (6 discs, 0307283704, 4 cassettes, 0307283690).

Obtaining Taped Materials for Students With Disabilities

Handicapped students may obtain assistance through the Books-on-Tape services provided by Recordings for the Blind and Dyslexic. Institutions may apply for membership. Students who apply for an individual membership pay a one-time $35 application fee. Applications will ask for a verification of a disability. Information about the RFB&D program, its eligibility requirements, and applications for service are available from

http://www.rfbd.org
Recording for the Blind and Dyslexic
20 Roszel Road
Princeton, NJ 08540
custserv@rfbd.org

Talking Books is a program of the United States Library of Congress that loans books, magazines, and four-track tape recorders to people not able to read conventional print. A physician is required to verify the child receiving service has a learning disability. For more information and an application visit

http://www.loc.gov/nls
National Library Service for the Blind and Physically Handicapped
Library of Congress
Washington, DC 20542
nls@loc.gov

http://www.talkingtapes.org
Talking Tapes
16 Sunnen Drive, Suite 162
St. Louis, MO 63143
1-877-926-0500
info@talkingtapes.org

Books Aloud, Inc. is a nonprofit organization that loans books on tape free to members living in the United States. Individuals who are blind, visually impaired, physically disabled, or learning disabled and are unable to read conventional print, hold a book, or turn the pages are eligible. For an application and verification of disability form visit

http://www.booksaloud.org
Books Aloud Inc.
P.O. Box 5731
San Jose, CA 95150
booksaloud@juno.com

Audio Books for All YA Readers

Why use audio books?

- As a whole class listen to 10-15 minutes of an audio book each day
  - o Read-aloud techniques that doesn't strain your voice after five class periods.
  - o Keeps the reading fresh for each class.
  - o Models fluent reading.
  - o Promotes a technique students might employ on their own.
- Assists students with reading disabilities regardless of severity.
- Allows less-able readers to engage in discussions with heterogeneously grouped classmates.
- Assist in building reading confidence and help build life-long readers.

Companies that provide quality audio books:

Recorded Books, LLC
270 Skipjack Road
Prince Frederick, MD 20678
1-800-638-1304
http://www.recordedbooks.com

Full Cast Audio
PO Box 6110
Syracuse, NY 13217
1-800-871-7411
http://www.fullcastaudio.com

Listening Library
1-800-726-0600
http://www.listeninglibrary.com

> Promote adherence to copyright laws. In most cases it is illegal to either copy a CD or cassette (exceptions are sometimes made for archival, non-circulating copies) unless you have a license or permission to do so. Archive your written permission.
> Consult "Quick Guide to Copyright" online at:
> http://www.esc4.net/instructional/copyright/copyright.htm or consult Carol Simpson's book, *Copyright for Schools* (Linworth).

 Fact or Fiction?—Cassette Tapes, CD, DVDs

Cassettes hold more information than CDs.

FACT: Cassettes are regularly loaded with up to 105 minutes of programming while CDs are only loaded with 74 minutes of programming. So a 6-hour tape would only use 4 cassettes while the same amount of time would require 5 CDs. Many producers are now looking to using DVDs for their products.

Cassette tapes are more durable than CDs.

FICTION: For the most part they have equal durability. A tape will warp if left in the sun, for example, while CDs basically last forever and are difficult to damage. A CD left in the sun does not matter. They are quite durable and can be dropped without damage. Dropping a cassette doesn't usually damage the tape. But running over a tape or a CD with a car is not recommended. Same with a DVD—care similar to that necessary for a CD is needed.

Users can hold a place more easily with a tape.

FICTION: While it's easy to hold a spot on a tape if you simply don't rewind or forward, a user can return to the exact spot on an audiotape. The same is true for a CD if you do not remove the CD from the player. If you leave the CD in the player (whether or not the player is turned off or on) the player will return to the exact spot when it is restarted.

Most cassette players have counters on them and thus cassette tapes are more convenient to find a particular spot than a CD.

FICTION: This is fiction for two reasons. Many inexpensive personal cassette players do not have counters, making it very labor intensive to use a tape for more than one class in a day. For example, using an audio tape for a read-aloud for 2 or more classes means the user must repeatedly spend time rewinding to an exact spot (which is a trial and error method) and stopping at a precise time as well. A counter does help if a counter is available. On the other hand, CDs have tracks that can easily provide a specific starting point—all you need to know is the track number.

DVDs will replace CDs that will ultimately completely replace audio cassette tapes.

FICTION: We do know that no American manufacturers are any longer producing the blank audio cassette tapes. Experts in the field are predicting that not only will CDs be replaced but so will DVDs as the availability of downloads and streaming becomes more prevalent. Read "Will CDs and DVDs Disappear?" by Peter Cohen (Online)
http://www.pcworld.com/article/id,112279-page,1/article.html

Section 7

Award Winners

Award Winners
Introduction

Awards for young adult books mirror the type of awards given to adult books and to those for children. Anyone winning a prestigious award, such as the Newbery or Printz award, is almost guaranteed to have a positive growth pattern in his or her financial situation. Some authors have said the awards have enabled them to quit their full-time job and to write full-time. That is true of Christopher Paul Curtis whose first two books, *The Watsons Go to Birmingham: 1963* (Delacorte, 1995) and *Bud, Not Buddy* (Delacorte, 1999) were named honor books and award winners both by the Newbery Committee and the Coretta Scott King Committee.

In 2006, the American Indian Library Association (AILA), an affiliate of the American Library Association (ALA), announced the very first of its American Indian Youth Literature Award. The new literary award was created to identify and honor the best writing and illustrating by and about American Indians. The awards are given in three categories: picture book, middle school, and young adult. This is the first major award for American Indian titles.

Students and teachers turn to these awards as an indication of quality or reader appeal. Awards have various goals and criteria for selection. Basically, there are two types of awards: the literary award or the popularity award. Most literary awards tend to disavow any reference of popularity to readers, but most choice (or popular) awards also give at least a token nod to the book's literary value. Literary awards that are given for a single title are often restricted to books published in a particular location within the past year while those given for the body of an author's work is comprehensive.

Choice awards are generally selected through a combination of checkpoints but are open to books published in a wider range of publication years—a span wide enough to ensure that the book has gained a certain degree of popularity and that the book could legitimately be considered in a choice list situation.

Literary awards tend to be sponsored by the American Library Association or one of its divisions. Choice awards are often sponsored by reading or library organizations based in specific states. A comprehensive list of specific state awards and links to their official sites is located at McBookwords: State and Regional Book Awards at http://www.mcelmeel.com/curriculum/bookawards.html

Book Awards

Literary Awards—Single Book

Awards that are given for a single title, based on the book's perceived literary value. A committee commissioned by the sponsoring organization or organizations often decides these awards. Most often the criteria for eligible books set time and place of publication criteria and criteria for the author/illustrator. Examples of this type of award include the John Newbery award, Michael L. Printz award, and the Golden Kite Award.

Literary Awards—Body of Work

Awards that are given for a single title, based on the book's perceived literary value. A committee commissioned by the sponsoring organization or organizations often decides these awards. Most often the criteria for eligible books set time and place of publication criteria and criteria for the author/illustrator. Examples of this type of award include the Margaret Edwards Award and the Hans Christian Anderson Award.

Choice Awards—Single Book

This award is often a combination of choices made by professional educators or authors and readers. This type of award is often sponsored by reading or librarian organizations that has a committee to choose the core list of books to be considered for the award. The appropriate readers then read the list and then choose and select the award winner.

The Michael L. Printz Award for
Excellence in Young Adult Literature

The Michael L. Printz Award is an award for a book that exemplifies literary excellence in young adult literature. It is named for a Topeka, Kansas school librarian who was a long-time active member of the Young Adult Library Services Association. The award is given annually by an award committee that can also name as many as four honor books. Fiction, non-fiction, poetry, or an anthology are eligible. Joint authors or editors are eligible as well. The books must be published between January 1 and December 31 of the preceding year and be designated by its publisher as being either a young adult book or one published for the age range that YALSA defines as young adult, ages 12 through 18.

Printz Award

2006	*Looking for Alaska*	John Green	Dutton
2005	*how i live now*	Meg Rosoff	Wendy Lamb/Random House
2004	*The First Part Last*	Angela Johnson	S&S
2003	*Postcards from No Man's Land*	Aidan Chambers	Dutton
2002	*A Step from Heaven*	An Na	Front Street
2001	*Kit's Wilderness*	David Almond	Delacorte
2000	*Monster*	Walter Dean Myers	HarperCollins

Printz Honor Award

2006	*Black Juice*	Margo Lanagan	EOS/HarperCollins
	I Am the Messenger	Markus Zusak	Alfred A. Knopf
	John Lennon: All I Want Is the Truth, a Photographic Biography	Elizabeth Partridge	Viking
	A Wreath for Emmett Till	Marilyn Nelson	Houghton Mifflin
2005	*Airborn*	Kenneth Oppel	Harpercollins
	Chanda's Secrets	Allan Stratton	Annick Press
	Lizzie Bright and the Buckminster Boy	Gary D. Schmidt	Clarion

2004	*A Northern Light*	Jennifer Donnelly	Harcourt
	Keesha's House	Helen Frost	FSG
	Fat Kid Rules the World	K.L. Going	Putnam
	The Earth, My Butt and Other Big Round Things	Carolyn Mackler	Candlewick
2003	*Postcards from No Man's Land*	Aidan Chambers	Dutton
	The House of the Scorpion	Nancy Farmer	S&S/Richard Jackson
	My Heartbeat	Garret Freymann-Weyr	Houghton
	Hole in My Life	Jack Gantos	FSG
2002	*The Ropemaker*	Peter Dickinson	Delacorte
	Heart to Heart: New Poems Inspired by Twentieth-Century American Art	Jan Greenberg	Abrams
	Freewill	Chris Lynch	HarperCollins
	True Believer	Virginia Euwer Wolff	Atheneum
2001	*Many Stones*	Carolyn Coman	Front Street
	The Body of Christopher Creed	Carol Plum-Ucci	Harcourt
	Angus, Thongs, and Full-Frontal Snogging	Louise Rennison	HarperCollins
	Stuck in Neutral	Terry Trueman	HarperCollins
2000	*Hard Love*	Ellen Wittlinger	S&S
	Skelling	David Almond	Delacorte
	Speak	Laura Halse Anderson	FSG

The John Newbery Award

The John Newbery Medal is awarded annually to the author of the most distinguished contribution to American literature for children published in English and in the United States during the preceding year. There are no limitations as to the character of the book considered except that it must be original work. Books that are also truly distinguished are named as Honor Books. The author must be a U.S. citizen or a resident.

Newbery Award

2006	*Criss Cross*	Lynne Rae Perkins	Greenwillow
2005	*Kira Kira*	Cynthia Kadohata	Atheneum
2004	*The Tale of Despereaux: Being the Story of a Mouse, a Princess, Some Soup, and a Spool of Thread*	Kate DiCamillo	Candlewick
2003	*Crispin: The Cross of Lead*	Avi	Hyperion
2002	*A Single Shard*	Linda Sue Park	Clarion
2001	*A Year Down Yonder*	Richard Peck	Dial
2000	*Bud, Not Buddy*	Christopher Paul Curtis	Delacorte

Newbery Honor Award

2006	*Whittington*	Alan Armstrong	Random House
	Hitler Youth: Growing Up in Hitler's Shadow	Susan Campbell Bartoletti	Scholastic Nonfiction
	Princess Academy	Shannon Hale	Bloomsbury
	Show Way	Jacqueline Woodson	G.P. Putnam
2005	*Al Capone Does My Shorts*	Gennifer Choldenko	Putnam
	Voice That Challenged a Nation: Marian Anderson and the Struggle for Equal Rights	Russell Freedman	Clarion
	Lizzie Bright and the Buckminster Boy	Gary D. Schmidt	Clarion
2004	*Olive's Ocean*	Kevin Henkes	Greenwillow Books
	An American Plague: The True and Terrifying Story of the Yellow Fever Epidemic of 1793	Jim Murphy	Clarion

Newbery Honor Award (cont.)

2003	*Pictures of Hollis Woods*	Patricia Reilly Giff	Random House/Wendy Lamb Books
	The House of the Scorpion	Nancy Farmer	S&S/Richard Jackson
	Hoot	Carl Hiaasen	Knopf
	A Corner of the Universe	Ann M. Martin	Scholastic
	Surviving the Applewhites	Stephanie S. Tolan	HarperCollins
2002	*Everything on a Waffle*	Polly Horvath	FSG
	Carver: A Life in Poems	Marilyn Nelson	Front Street
2001	*Hope Was Here*	Joan Bauer	G. P. Putnam
	Because of Winn-Dixie	Kate DiCamillo	Candlewick
	Joey Pigza Loses Control	Jack Gantos	FSG
	The Wanderer	Sharon Creech	Joanna Cotler Books/HarperCollins
2000	*Getting Near to Baby*	Audrey Couloumbis	Putnam
	Our Only May Amelia	Jennifer L. Holm	HarperCollins
	26 Fairmount Avenue	Tomie dePaola	Putnam

American Indian Youth Literature Award

The American Indian Youth Literature Award is an award for a book that exemplifies literary excellence that also identifies and honors the very best writing and illustrating by and about American Indians. Books selected to receive the award present Native Americans in the fullness of their humanity in the present and past contexts. Of the three categories in which the award is given, the middle school category and the young adult category will be of interest to those readers in the grade 6–12 age range.

American Indian Youth Literature Award

2006 Young Adult	*Hidden Roots*	Joseph Bruchac	Scholastic, 2004; 2006
2006 Middle School	*The Birchbark House*	Louise Erdrich	Hyperion, 1999; 2002

Pura Belpré Award

The Pura Belpré Award, established in 1996, is presented to a latino/latina writer and illustrator whose work best portrays, affirms, and celebrates the Latino cultural experience in an outstanding work of literature for children and youth.

The award is named after Pura Belpré, the first Latina librarian from the New York Public Library. As a children's librarian, storyteller, and author, she enriched the lives of Puerto Rican children in the U.S.A. through her pioneering work of preserving and disseminating Puerto Rican folklore. The award, given biennially, is co-sponsored by the Association for Library Service to Children (ALSC), a division of the American Library Association (ALA), and the National Association to Promote Library and Information Services to Latinos and the Spanish-Speaking (REFORMA), an ALA Affiliate.

Pura Belpré Award for Narrative

2006	*The Tequila Worm*	Viola Canales	Wendy Lamb/ Random House 2005
2004	*Before We Were Free*	Julia Alvarez	Alfred A. Knopf, 2002
2002	*Esperanza Rising*	Pam Munoz Ryan	Scholastic Press, 2000
2000	*Under the Royal Palms: A Childhood in Cuba*	Alma Flor Ada	Atheneum Books, 1998

Pura Belpré Honor Award for Narrative

2006	*César: ¡Sí, Se Puede! Yes, We Can!*	Carmen T. Bernier-Grand	Marshall Cavendish 2005
	Doña Flor: A Tall Tale About a Giant Woman with a Great Big Heart	Pat Mora	Alfred A. Knopf 2005
	Becoming Naomi León	Pam Muñoz Ryan	Scholastic Press 2004
2004	*Cuba 15*	Nancy Osa	Delacorte, 2003
	My Diary from Here to There/Mi Diario de Aquí Hasta Allá	Amada Irma Pérez	Children's Book Press
2002	*Breaking Through*	Francisco Jiménez	Houghton Mifflin, 2001
	Iguanas in the Snow (Picture Book)	Francisco X. Alarcón	Children's Book Press
2000	*From the Bellybutton of the Moon and Other Summer Poems/ Del Ombligo de la Luna y Otro Poemas de Verano. (Picture Book)*	Francisco X. Alarcón	Children's Book Press, 1998
	Laughing out Loud, I Fly: Poems in English and Spanish	Juan Felipe Herrera	HarperCollins, 1998

Coretta Scott King Award
& John Steptoe New Talent Award

The Coretta Scott King Award is presented annually by the Coretta Scott King Task Force of the American Library Association's Ethnic Multicultural Information Exchange Round Table (EMIERT). Recipients are authors and illustrators of African descent whose distinguished books promote an understanding and appreciation of the "American Dream." The Coretta Scott King Award jury also chooses the winners of the John Steptoe Award for New Talent Award winners. These books affirm new talent and offer visibility to excellence in writing or illustration at the beginning of a career as a published book creator.

Coretta Scott King Award

2006	*Day of Tears: A Novel in Dialogue*	Julius Lester	Jump at the Sun
2005	*Remember: The Journey to School Integration*	Toni Morrison	Houghton Mifflin
2004	*The First Part Last*	Angela Johnson	S&S
2003	*Bronx Masquerade*	Nikki Grimes	Dial
2002	*The Land*	Mildred Taylor	Phyllis Fogelman/Penguin Putnam
2001	*Miracle's Boys*	Jacqueline Woodson	G.P. Putnam's Sons
2000	*Bud, Not Buddy*	Christopher Paul Curtis	Delacorte

Coretta Scott King Honor Award

2006	*Maritcha: A Nineteenth-Century American Girl*	Tonya Bolden	Harry N. Abrams
	Dark Sons	Nikki Grimes	Hyperion Books for Children
	A Wreath for Emmett Till	Marilyn Nelson	Houghton Mifflin
2005	*Fortune's Bones: The Manumission Requiem*	Marilyn Nelson	Front Street
	Who Am I Without Him? Short Stories About Girls and Boys in Their Lives	Sharon G. Flake	Farrar Straus Giroux
	The Legend of Buddy Bush	Shelia P. Moses	Margaret K McElderry/Simon & Schuster
2004	*Days of Jubilee: The End of Slavery in the United States (Scholastic)*	Patricia C. and Fredrick L. McKissack	Scholastic

	Locomotion	Jacqueline Woodson	G.P. Putnams's Son
	The Battle of Jericho	Sharon M. Draper	Atheneum
2003	***The Red Rose Box***	Brenda Woods	G.P. Putnam's
	Talkin' About Bessie: the Story of Aviator Elizabeth Coleman	Nikki Grimes (also Illustration Award for E.B. Lewis)	Orchard Books/Scholastic
2002	*Money-Hungry*	Sharon G. Flake	Jump at the Sun/Hyperion
	Carver: A Life in Poems by Marilyn Nelson (Front Street)	Marilyn Nelson	Front Street
2001	***Let It Shine! Stories of Black Women Freedom Fighters***	Andrea Davis Pinkney	Gulliver Books, Harcourt
2000	*Francie*	Karen English	FSG
	Monster by Walter Dean Myers (HarperCollins)	Walter Dean Myers	HarperCollins
	Black Hands, White Sails: The Story of African-American	Patricia C. McKissack and Fredrick L. McKissack	Scholastic

John Steptoe New Talent Award

The winner may not have published more than three books and may only receive the award once. If the book is selected for the Coretta Scott King Award it is not eligible for the new talent award. There is one award for writing and a second for illustration, if appropriate. If no book is qualified, the award need not be given in that particular year.

2006	**Jimi & Me**	Jaime Adoff	Jump at the Sun
2005	*Missy Violet and Me*	Author: Barbara Hathaway	Houghton Mifflin
2004	*The Way a Door Closes*	Author: Hope Anita Smith	Henry Holt
2003	*Chill Wind*	Author: Janet McDonald	Frances Foster Books/FSG
2002	**no author award presented**		
2001	**no awards presented**		
2000	**no awards presented**		

Golden Kite Award

Since 1973 the Society of Children's Book Writers and Illustrators (SCBWI) has presented this award to several of their peers. This award is coveted as it is the only award given to a writer or illustrator by his or her peers. The award is presented annually in four categories: fiction, nonfiction, picture book text, and picture book illustration. (2006 awards will be announced in April 2007; awards are accepted at the SCBWI's annual conference in August.)

2006 Fiction			
2006 nonfiction			
2005 Fiction	*A Room on Lorelei Street*	Mary E. Pearson	Henry Holt
2005 nonfiction	*Children of the Great Depression*	Russell Freedman	Clarion
2004 Fiction	*Bucking the Sarge*	Christopher Paul Curtis	Wendy Lamb
2004 nonfiction	*Dust to Eat: Drought and Depression in the 1930s*	Michael L. Cooper	Clarion
2003 Fiction	*Milkweed*	Jerry Spinelli	Alfred A. Knopf/Random House
2003 nonfiction	*Leonardo: Beautiful Dreamer*	Robert Byrd	Dutton/Penguin
2002 Fiction	*Fresh Girl*	Jaïra Placide	Random House/Wendy Lamb
2002 nonfiction	*This Land Was Made for You and Me: The Life and Songs of Woody Guthrie*	Elizabeth Partridge	Viking
2001 Fiction	*True Believer*	Virginia Euwer Wolff	Atheneum
2001 nonfiction	*Black Potatoes: The Story of the Great Irish Famine*	Susan Campbell Bartoletti	Houghton Mifflin
2000 Fiction	*The Boxer*	Kathleen Karr	FSG
2000 nonfiction	*Darkness Over Denmark*	Ellen Levine	Holiday House

Golden Kite Honor Award

Year / Type	Title	Author	Publisher
2006 Fiction			
2006 nonfiction			
2005 Fiction	*Each Little Bird That Sings*	Deborah Wiles	Harcourt, Inc.
2005 nonfiction	*The Forbidden Schoolhouse: The True and Dramatic Story of Prudence Crandall and Her Students*	Suzanne Jurmain	Houghton Mifflin
2004 Fiction	*Bucking the Sarge*	Christopher Paul Curtis	Wendy Lamb Books
2004 nonfiction	*The Power of One: Daisy Bates and the Little Rock Nine*	Judith Bloom Fradin & Dennis Fradin	Clarion
2003 Fiction	*Breath*	Donna Jo Napoli	Atheneum/S&S
2003 nonfiction	*After the Last Dog Died: The True-Life, Hair-Raising Adventure of Douglas Mawson and His 1911-1914 Antarctic Expedition*	Carmen Bredeson	National Geographic
2002 Fiction	*Shaper*	Jessie Haas	Greenwillow
2002 nonfiction	*Ansel Adams: America's Photographer*	Beverly Gherman	Little, Brown
2001 Fiction	*The Life History of a Star*	Kelly Easton	Margaret K. McElderry
2001 nonfiction	*John & Abigail Adams: An American Love Story*	Judith St. George	Holiday House
2000 Fiction	*Nory Ryan's Song*	Patricia Reilly Giff	Delacorte Press
2000 nonfiction	*Fireflies in the Dark: The Story of Freid Dicker-Brandies and the Children of Terezin*	Susan Goldman Rubin	Holiday House

National Book Award

The National Book Awards have been given for the past 55 years. There are four categories: fiction, nonfiction, poetry, and young people's literature. The Young People's section was added in 1996.

Announced in November of each year.

2006			
2005	*The Penderwicks*	Jeanne Birdsall	Alfred A. Knopf
2004	*Godless*	Paul Hautman	Simon & Schuster
2003	*The Canning Season*	Polly Horvath	
2002	*The House of the Scorpion*	Nancy Farmer	
2001	*True Believer*	Virginia Euwer Wolff	
2000	*Homeless Bird*	Gloria Whelan	

Books on the short list for the 2005 award included:
- ❑ Adele Griffin, *Where I Want to Be* (Putnam)
- ❑ Chris Lynch, *Inexcusable* (Atheneum)
- ❑ Walter Dean Myers, *Autobiography of My Dead Brother* (HarperTempest)
- ❑ Deborah Wiles, *Each Little Bird That Sings* (Harcourt)

Books on the short list for the 2004 award included:
- ❑ Deb Caletti, *Honey, Baby, Sweetheart* (Simon & Schuster Books for Young Readers)
- ❑ Laban Carrick Hill, *Harlem Stomp!: A Cultural History of the Harlem Renaissance* (Megan Tingley Books/Little, Brown & Company)
- ❑ Shelia P. Moses, *The Legend of Buddy Bush* (Margaret K. McElderry Books/Simon & Schuster Children's Publishing Division)
- ❑ Julie Anne Peters, *Luna: A Novel* (Megan Tingley Books/Little, Brown & Company)

Books on the short list for the 2003 award included:
- ❑ Paul Fleischman, *Breakout*, Cricket Books/A Marcato Book/Carus Publishing Company.
- ❑ Polly Horvath, *The Canning Season*, Farrar, Straus & Giroux;
- ❑ Jim Murphy, *An American Plague: The True and Terrifying Story of the Yellow Fever Epidemic of 1793*, Clarion Books/Houghton Mifflin;
- ❑ Richard Peck, *The River Between Us*, Dial Books/Penguin Group USA,
- ❑ Jacqueline Woodson, *Locomotion*, G.P. Putnam Sons/Penguin Group USA.

Robert F. Siebert Information Book Award

Established in 2001, the Association of Library Service to Children (ALSC) presents this award annually to the author of the most distinguished information book published in the previous year. The award is named after Robert F. Sibert, a long-time president of Bound-to-Stay Bound Books. That company sponsors the award.

Robert F. Siebert Information Book Award

Year	Title	Author	Publisher
2006	*Secrets of a Civil War Submarine: Solving the Mysteries of the H.L. Hunley*	*Sally M. Walker*	Carolrhoda
2005	*The Voice that Challenged a Nation: Marian Anderson and the Struggle for Equal Rights*	*Russell Freedman*	Clarion
2004	*An American Plague: The True and Terrifying Story of the Yellow Fever Epidemic of 1793*	Jim Murphy	Clarion
2003	*Life & Death of Adolf Hitler*	James Cross Giblin	Houghton Mifflin
2002	*Black Potatoes: The Story of the Great Irish Famine*	Susan Campbell Bartoletti	
2001	*Sir Walter Raleigh & the Quest for El Dorado*	Marc Aronson	

Robert F. Siebert Information Book Honor Award

Year	Title	Author	Publisher
2006	*Hitler Youth: Growing Up in Hitler's Shadow*	Susan Campbell Bartoletti	Scholastic Nonfiction
2005	*Sequoyah: The Cherokee Man Who Gave His People Writing*	James Rumford	Houghton Mifflin
	The Tarantula Scientist	Sy Montgomery	Houghton Mifflin
	Walt Whitman: Words for America	Barbara Kerley	Scholastic
2004	*no YA titles named as honor books*		
2003	*Six Days in October: The Stock Market Crash of 1929*	Karen Blumenthal	Atheneum
	Hole in My Life	Jack Gantos	FSG
	Action Jackson	Jan and Jordan Greenberg	Millbrook Press
	When Marian Sings	Pam Munoz Ryan	Scholastic
2002	*Surviving Hitler: A Boy in he Nazi Death Camps*	Andrea Warren	
	Vincent Van Gogh	Jan Greenberg & Sandra Jordan	
	Brooklyn Bridge	Lynn Curlee	
2001	*Longitude Prize*	Joan Dash	
	Blizzard! The Storm that Changed America	Jim Murphy	
	My Season with Penguins: An Antarctic Journal	Sophie Webb	
	Pedro and Me: Friendship, Loss, & What I Learned	Judd Winick	

Schneider Family Book Award

The Schneider Family Book Award is given to an author or illustrator for a book that portrays some aspect of living with a disability or a disability of a friend or family member. The disability may be physical, mental, or emotional. Winners in three categories, books for birth through grade school (approx. ages 0–10), middle school [11–13], and teens (age 13-18), are given $5000 and a framed plaque. Books must have been published in the past three years and be created by a United States author or illustrator. The American Library Association administers the award.

2006 Teen	*Under the Wolf, Under the Dog*	Adam Rapp	Candlewick
2006 Middle	*Tending to Grace*	Kimberly Newton Fusco	Alfred A. Knopf
2005 Teen	*My Thirteenth Winter: A Memoir*	Samantha Abeel	Orchard
2005 Middle	*Becoming Naomi León*	Pam Muñoz Ryan	Scholastic
2004 Teen	*Things Not Seen*	Andrew Clements	Philomel, 2002
2004 Middle	*A Mango-Shaped Space*	Wendy Mass	Little Brown, 2003

The W. Y. Boyd Literary Award

"For Excellence in Military Fiction"

These books are not necessarily YA books but may be suitable.

The W Y. Boyd Award is given for the best fiction set in a period when the United States was at war. The book must have been published in the prior year. It recognizes the service of American veterans and military personnel and encourages the writing and publishing of outstanding war-related fiction. The American Library Association administers the award.

2006	*Articles of War*	Nick Arvin	Doubleday
2005	*To the Last Man: A Novel of the First World War*	Jeff Shaara	Ballantine
2004	*Glory in the Name: A Novel of the Confederate Navy*	James L. Nelson	HarperCollins
2003	*Warning of War*	James Brady	St. Martin's Press
2002	*Sharkman Six*	Simon & Schuster	Simon & Schuster
2001	*Dog Company Six*	Brigadier General Edwin Howard Simmons	Naval Institute Press
2000	*Soldier in Paradise*	John Mort	Soldier in Paradise

Young Adult Library Services Association (YALSA) 2006 Alex Awards

YALSA and *Booklist* announce the list of "ALEX" books as part of National Library Week (third week of April) each year. The titles are "outstanding adult fiction and non-fiction titles that will intrigue and challenge the diverse audience of teen readers."

- ❑ Bates, Judy Fong. *Midnight at the Dragon Café*. Counterpoint. (1582431892)
- ❑ Buckhanon, Kalisha. *Upstate*. St Martins. (0312332688)
- ❑ Gaiman, Neil. *Anansi Boys*. William Morrow & Company. (006051518x)
- ❑ Galloway, Gregory. *As Simple As Snow*. Putnam. (0399152318)
- ❑ Ishiguro, Kazuo. *Never Let Me Go*. Alfred A. Knopf. (1400043395)
- ❑ Martinez, A. Lee. *Gil's All Fright Diner*. Tor. (076531711)
- ❑ Palwick, Susan. *The Necessary Beggar*. Tor. (076531097x)
- ❑ Rawles, Nancy. *My Jim*. Crown. (1400054001)
- ❑ Scheeres, Julia. *Jesus Land: A Memoir*. Counterpoint. (152433380)
- ❑ Walls, Jeannette. *The Glass Castle: A Memoir*. Scribner. (0743247531)

2005 Alex Awards

- ❑ Almond, Steve. *Candyfreak: A Journey through the Chocolate Underbelly of America*. Algonquin Books of Chapel Hill. (1565124129).
- ❑ Cox, Lynn. *Swimming to Antarctica: Tales of a Long-Distance Swimmer*. Knopf. (0375415076).
- ❑ Halpin, Brendan. *Donorboy*. Random House. (1400062772).
- ❑ Kurson, Robert. *Shadow Divers*. Random House. (0375508589).
- ❑ Meyers, Kent. *Work of Wolves*. Harcourt. (0151010579).
- ❑ Patchett, Ann. *Truth & Beauty: A Friendship*. HarperCollins. (0060572140).
- ❑ Picoult, Jodi. *My Sister's Keeper*. Atria. (0743454529).
- ❑ Reed, Kit. *Thinner Than Thou*. Tom Doherty Associates. (0765307626).
- ❑ Shepard, Jim. *Project X*. Knopf. (140004071X).
- ❑ Sullivan, Robert. *Rats: Observations on the History and Habitat of the City's Most Unwanted Inhabitants*. Bloomsbury. (1582343853).

The Margaret A. Edwards Award
for Lifetime Achievement

The Margaret A. Edwards Award, established in 1988, honors an author's lifetime achievement for writing books that have been popular over a period of time. The annual award is administered by YALSA and sponsored by School Library Journal magazine.

Presented annually since 1990.

2006—Jacqueline Woodson, cited for givng voice to outsiders often invisible to mainstream America: *I Hadn't Meant to Tell You This, Lena, From the Notebooks of Melanin Sun, If You Come Softly,* and *Miracle's Boys*.

2005—Francesca Lia Block, cited for her ground-breaking *Weetzie Bat* books: *Weetzie Bat; Witch Baby; Cherokee Bat and the Goat Guys; Missing Angel Juan;* and *Baby Be-Bop*.

2004—Ursula K. Le Guin, cited for *A Wizard of Earthsea; The Tombs of Atuan; The Farthest Shore; Tehanu; The Left Hand of Darkness;* and *The Beginning Place*.

2003—Nancy Garden, cited for *Annie On My Mind*.

2002—Paul Zindel, cited for *The Pigman; The Pigman's Legacy; The Pigman & Me; My Darling, My Hamburger;* and *The Effect of Gamma Rays on Man-in-the-Moon Marigolds: A Drama in Two Acts*.

2001—Robert Lipsyte, cited for *The Contender; The Brave; The Chief;* and *One Fat Summer*.

2000—Chris Crutcher, cited for *Staying Fat for Sarah Byrnes; Athletic Shorts; Chinese Handcuffs; The Crazy Horse Electric Game; Stotan!;* and *Running Loose*.

1999—Anne McCaffrey, cited for the series *Dragonriders of Pern,* comprising *Dragonflight, Dragonquest*, and the *White Dragon. The Ship Who Sang* and the Harper Hall Trilogy: *Dragonsong, Dragonsinger, and Dragondrums*

1998—Madeleine L'Engle, cited for the Austin Family Series, which includes *Meet the Austins* and *A Ring of Endless Light;* and the Time Fantasy Series, which includes *A Wrinkle In Time* and *A Swiftly Tilting Planet*.

1997—Gary Paulsen, cited for *Hatchet; Woodsong; Winter Room; The Crossing; Canyons;* and *Dancing Carl*.

1996—Judy Blume, cited for *Forever*.

1995—Cynthia Voigt, cited for *Homecoming; Dicey's Song; Solitary Blue; Building Blocks; The Runner; Jackaroo;* and *Izzy, Willy-Nilly*.

For a complete list, visit www.ala.org/yalsa/edwards/

McElmeel's Significant Books
A List of Fifty

In no particular order

- ❑ Lewis Carroll, *Alice's Adventures in Wonderland*
- ❑ JRR Tolkien, *The Hobbit*
- ❑ Dodie Smith, *I Capture the Castle*
- ❑ J.K. Rowling, *Harry Potter and the Sorcerer's Stone*
- ❑ S.E. Hinton, *The Outsiders*
- ❑ Madeleine L'Engle, *A Wrinkle in Time*
- ❑ Margaret Mahy, *The Changeover*
- ❑ David Almond, *Skellig*
- ❑ Michael Chabon, *Summerland*
- ❑ Nancy Farmer, *A Girl Named Disaster*
- ❑ Joan Abelove, *Go and Come Back*
- ❑ Naomi Shihab Nye, *Habibi*
- ❑ Virginia Euwer Wolff, *Make Lemonade* (and sequels)
- ❑ Robert Cormier, *The Chocolate War*
- ❑ Walter Dean Myers, *Fallen Angels*
- ❑ Jacqueline Woodson, *Locomotion*
- ❑ Joan Bauer, *Squashed*
- ❑ Norma Howe, *Adventures of Blue Avenger*
- ❑ Patrice Kindl, *Owl in Love*
- ❑ Anne Fine, *Flour Babies*
- ❑ Julie Anne Peters, *Define Normal*
- ❑ Angela Johnson, *Toning the Sweep*
- ❑ Annette Curtis Klause, *The Silver Kiss (Blood and Chocolate)*
- ❑ M.E. Kerr, *Night Kites*
- ❑ Francesca Lia Block, *Weetzie Bat*
- ❑ Philip Pullman, *The Golden Compass (The Ruby and the Smoke)*
- ❑ Donna Jo Napoli, *Beast* or *Zel*
- ❑ Neil Gaiman, *Coraline*
- ❑ Terry Pratchett, *Wee Free Men*
- ❑ Robert O'Brien, *Z for Zachariah*
- ❑ Peter S. Beagle, *Tamsin*
- ❑ Nina Kiriki Hoffman, *A Stir of Bones*
- ❑ *Firebirds*, edited by Sharyn November

- Michael Rosen, *Shakespeare: His Work and His World*
- Marilyn Nelson, *Carver: A life in poems*
- Robie H. Harris, illus Michael Emberley, *It's Perfectly Normal*
- Kathleen Krull, *Lives of Extraordinary Women: Rulers, Rebels and What the Neighbors Thought* (or any others in her series of collective biographies)
- Maria Testa, *Becoming Joe DiMaggio*
- Gary Paulsen, *How Angel Peterson Got His Name*
- Rob Thomas, *Rats Saw God*
- Melvin Burgess, *Doing It*
- Chris Crutcher, *Staying Fat for Sarah Byrnes*
- Louis Sachar, *Holes*
- Maureen Daly, *Seventeenth Summer*
- Per Nilsson, *Heart's Delight*
- Garret Freymann-Weyr, *My Heartbeat*
- Mildred Taylor, *Roll of Thunder, Hear my Cry*
- M.T. Anderson, *Feed*
- Carl Hiassen, *Hoot*
- Paul Fleischman, *Seek*

Why are these books significant?
How many do you know?
What five titles would you add?

Words from Bibliophiles

"When I get a little money, I buy books; and, if any is left, I buy food and clothes."—Erasmus

"Time spent reading, like time spent loving, increases our lifetime."—Daniel Pennac

"Some books are undeservedly forgotten, none are undeservedly remembered."—W.H. Auden

"Libraries are reservoirs of strength, grace and wit, reminders of order, calm and continuity, lakes of mental energy, neither warm nor cold, light nor dark..."—Germaine Greer

"When an old man dies, a library burns to the ground."—African Proverb

"Anyone who says they have only one life to live must not know how to read a book."—Anonymous

"I have always imagined that Paradise will be a kind of library."—Jorge Luis Borges

"The library is the temple of learning, and learning has liberated more people than all the wars in history."—Carl Rowan

"I am a part of everything I have read."—John Kieran

"A book must be an ice ax to break the frozen sea within us."—Franz Kafka

"Outside of a dog, a book is a man's best friend. Inside of a dog, it's too dark to read."—Groucho Marx

"People say that life's the thing, but I prefer reading."—Logan P. Smith

"No story ever really ends, and I think I know why."—George MacDonald

"A house without books is like a room without windows."—Horace Mann

"When you sell a person a book you don't sell just twelve ounces of paper and ink and glue; you sell a whole new life."—Christopher Morley

Section 8

Theme Lists and Book Packages

Theme Lists and Book Packages
Introduction

If you subscribe to the fact that readers learn more effectively when they already know something about a topic, you will want to consider "pairing" or creating book packages of books for readers to read. Experiences or having read one book help to build concepts in a particular area that mean something to them and to their particular background or culture. When a second book is linked to that first book, the link helps the reader take in new information to complement their prior knowledge. The reader's interest and curiosity are activated, and activities relating to either one of the books are infused with a sense of purpose. Some refer to this pairing (which may limit the selections to just two) or packaging as "bundling," which could conceivably include any number of titles but most often includes 4–5 titles that relate in some way. The packaging of related titles need not be non-fiction with fiction; for example, the packaging might be several books of fiction with a similar theme, focus, or setting. Other types of packages are appropriate as well: fiction with non-fiction; fiction with fiction; non-fiction with non-fiction; fiction with film; non-fiction with film; and so forth.

Longer lists are generally referred to as "thematic lists." By using one book (a familiar title perhaps) to activate a reader's prior knowledge, the stage can be set for enhancing comprehension, for setting a purpose for reading/listening, and for providing new meaningful and challenging experiences and a new reading.

The annotations with the books in the book packages that follow should help readers determine the "package" theme that will correlate with curriculum or interests of specific readers.

Ellen & William Craft (and Slavery)
Connect non-fiction, short stories, full-length historical fiction

- ❑ Fradin, Judith Bloom and Dennis Brindell Fradin. *5,000 Miles to Freedom: Ellen and William Craft's Flight From Slavery*. (2006) National Geographic. (0792278852).

- ❑ Lester, Julius. *This Strange New Feeling: Three Love Stories from Black History*. (1982; 2006) Dial. (0803731728)

- ❑ Lester, Julius. *Day of Tears: A Novel in Dialogue*. (2005) Hyperion/Jump at the Sun. (0786804904).

Immigrants—Crossing the Mexican Border
Connect personal narratives, historical fiction, non-fiction

- ❑ Beatty, Patricia. *Lupita Mañana*. (2000) HarperTrophy. (0380732475)

- ❑ Gallo, Donald R., ed. *First Crossing: Stories about Teen Immigrants*. (2004) Candlewick Press. (0763622494)

- ❑ Hobbs, Will. *Crossing the Wire*. (2006) HarperCollins. (0060741384).

- ❑ Nazario, Sonia. *Enrique's Journey*. (2006) Random House. (1400062055).

World War II—Snapshots of People and Events
Connect non-fiction and full-length historical fiction

- ❏ Borden, Louise. *The Journey That Saved Curious George: The True Wartime Escape of Margret and H. A. Rey*. (2005) Illustrated by Allan Drummond. Houghton Mifflin. (0618339248)

- ❏ Bruchac, Joseph. *Code Talker: A Novel About the Navajo Marines of World War Two.* (2005) Dial. (0803729219).

- ❏ Kadohata, Cynthia. *Weedflower*. (2006) Simon & Schuster/Atheneum. (0689865740).

- ❏ Oppenheim, Joanne. *Dear Miss Breed: True Stories of the Japanese American Incarceration During World War II and a Librarian Who Made a Difference*. (2006) Scholastic Nonfiction. (0439569923).

- ❏ Bartoletti, Susan Campbell. *Hitler Youth: Growing Up in Hitler's Shadow*. (2005) Scholastic. Illustrated with photographs. (0439353793).

Librarians – Books to Children
Connect non-fiction, full-length historical fiction, and picture books.

- ❏ Oppenheim, Joanne. *Dear Miss Breed: True Stories of the Japanese American Incarceration During World War II and a Librarian Who Made a Difference*. (2006) Scholastic Nonfiction. (0439569923).

- ❏ Appelt, Kathi. *Down Cut Shin Creek: The Pack Horse Librarians of Kentucky*. (2001) HarperCollins.

- ❏ Peck, Richard. *Here Lies the Librarian*. (2006) Dial.

- ❏ Ruurs, Margrite. *My Librarian Is a Camel: How Books Are Brought to Children Around the World.* (2005) Boyds Mills Press.

- ❏ Stamaty, Mark Alan. *Alia's Mission: Saving the Books of Iraq*. (2004) Knopf.

- ❏ Stotts, Stuart. *Books in Boxes: Lutie Stearns and the Traveling Libraries of Wisconsin*. (2005) Big Valley Press.

- ❏ Winter, Jeanette. *The Librarian of Basra: A True Story from Iraq*. (2005) Harcourt.

Sources for Magazine Lists

Madison Public Library List—Magazines for Kids and Teens
http://yahelp.suffolk.lib.ny.us/yamags.html

Magazine.com — a subscription service list for teens
http://www.magazines.com/ncom/mag?subject=0002

Online Magazines for Teens

ChristianityToday.com— http://www.christiancollegeguide.net/
A Christian perspective. Advice for teens on: love, sex, family relationships, self-image, popularity, loneliness and more, in regular columns, feature article and fiction.

CollegeBound Network—http://www.cbnet.com/
Information about getting into college, taking admissions exams, and more.

Computer Gaming World—http://cgw.1up.com/
"The #1 computer game magazine." Monthly updates.

Cyberteens —http://www.cyberteens.com/
Forums, stories, games, music, art, and shockwave movies produced by teens.

Devo'Zine—http://www.upperroom.org/devozine/
Inter-denominational devotional magazine for teens.

HiPMag Online—http://www.hipmag.org
Non-profit magazine for deaf and hard of hearing kids ages eight to fourteen.

Oasis—http://www.oasismag.com/
For and by lesbian, gay, bisexual, transgender, and questioning youth.

PC Gamer—http://www.pcgamer.com/
Demos, articles , interviews, game reviews and more.

React—http://www.react.com/
Stories, feature and column offer readers a chance to respond and interact.

Seventeen Online—http://www.seventeen.com/
Online version. Message boards, live chat, AOL's instant messenger.

Sex, Etc—http://www.sexetc.org or http://www.sxetc.org
Newsletter written by teens for teens on important health and sexuality issues. Published by The Network for Family Life Education, Rutgers University.

Spank!—http://www.spankmag.com/
Youth culture online. Focuses on youth issues, interests, and happenings, published monthly (with daily updates). Editorial Board volunteers from 14 to 28 and publishing professionals to ensure it remains focused on youth interests.

Teen—http://www.teenmag.com/
Beauty, fitness, advice, interviews, chat.

About the Author

Sharron L. McElmeel has built a national reputation as a resource for those interested in children's and young adult literature. In addition to having written more than two dozen books in the area of children's and young adult literature, she is an instructor at the University of Wisconsin-Stout and writes and edits for a number of educational publications. She has been named as Iowa Reading Teacher of the Year by the Iowa Reading Association, honored with the organization's Celebrate Literacy Award, nominated as Iowa's Teacher of the Year, and named one of the Top Ten Online Educators of the Year (2004). She is an often-requested speaker at conferences and professional development workshops. Each year she develops new presentations and topics but is willing to tailor a presentation toward the objectives you might have for your specific conference or curricular needs. Contact McBookwords by e-mail (mcelmeel@mcelmeel.com) or phone (319) 393-2562. More information is available online at www.mcelmeel.com

Popular Seminar—"The Best Teen Reads: 2007"
An energetic, informative seminar that expands on the material in the book, **The Best Teen Reads for 2007**.
mcelmeel@mcelmeel.com or phone (319) 393-2562

More Books by Sharron L. McElmeel

Authors in the Pantry: Recipes, Stories, and More. (2007) Libraries Unlimited. ISBN: 1591583217

100 Most Popular Children's Authors: Biographical Sketches and Bibliographies. (1999) Libraries Unlimited. ISBN: 1563086468

100 Most Popular Picture Books Authors and Illustrators: Biographical Sketches and Bibliographies. (2000) Libraries Unlimited. ISBN: 1563086476

ABCs of an Author/Illustrator Visit. 2nd edition. (2001) Linworth Publishers. ISBN: 1586830341

Authors in the Kitchen: Recipes, Stories, and More. (2005) Libraries Unlimited. ISBN: 15915823805

Character Education: A Book Guide for Teachers, Librarians, and Parents (2002) Libraries Unlimited. ISBN: 1563088843

Children's Authors and Illustrators Too Good to Miss (2004) Libraries Unlimited. ISBN: 1591580277

Literature Frameworks: From Apples to Zoos, 2nd edition. (2002) Linworth Publishers. ISBN: 1586830600

Index